Dan Rice, D.V.

Akit

Everythin
Feeding,

Filled with Full-color Photographs
Illustrations by Michele Earle-Bridges

BARRON'S

CONTENTS

ORIGIN OF THE AKITA

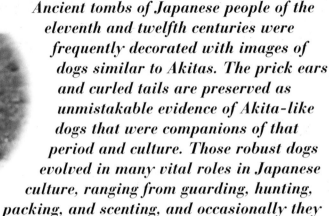

Ancient tombs of Japanese people of the eleventh and twelfth centuries were frequently decorated with images of dogs similar to Akitas. The prick ears and curled tails are preserved as unmistakable evidence of Akita-like dogs that were companions of that period and culture. Those robust dogs evolved in many vital roles in Japanese culture, ranging from guarding, hunting, packing, and scenting, and occasionally they were raised to provide meat for Japanese tables.

Akita History

Akitas were used for many different purposes. They were expected to guard the home of their masters and occasionally were pitted against other dogs and fought to the death for their masters' glory. They were taught to carry packs and pull sledges or carts. Akitas have been used to scent out and hunt down bears, boars, and other big game for their masters' tables and when times were hard, their lives were occasionally sacrificed to feed and clothe their human families.

Heritage

Akita heritage is steeped in history. They may have been developed from a cross between the Kari, the Tosa Fighting Dog, and several European breeds. Their presence may possibly date to

Akitas were once owned only by Japanese royalty.

5000 B.C. when they were brought to the Japanese islands from mainland China. Details of that history have been obscured by centuries of isolation on the remote Japanese island of Honshu, and sometimes it has been muddied by language and translation problems. Akita-like dogs, with tightly curled tails and erect ears, were evident in drawings and painting as early as 1150 A.D.

Contemporary Akitas

The contemporary Akita was developed in the 1630s by a Japanese feudal lord to hunt bear and other large game. The breed was known by Japanese royalty as *Matagi-inu*, the esteemed hunter. Ownership of an Akita was at one time limited to the rulers of Japan, who decked them out with special collars to designate the rank of the owner. They were treated to all the niceties—the best diet that Japanese royalty had to offer, and a special vocabulary

was used to address them. The Shogunate Hawk Chambers' records indicate that Akitas worked with hawks during boar and deer hunting.

A great deal of spiritual significance is attached to Akitas in their homeland and small statues of Akitas are commonly found in Japanese (and American) homes because they are symbols of good health.

For several hundred years Akitas' popularity rose and fell with the Japanese dynasties, depending on the habits and desires of the ruling classes. However, in the time of Emperor Taisho (1912–1926), dog fancy became quite popular. Following the styles of Great Britain, France, and Spain, Japanese dogs became a status symbol among the populace and royalty alike. European influence revived the interest in Akitas, and once again they gained importance in Japan and elsewhere as loyal companions and protectors of the home.

Odate Dogs

Akitas were originally known as Odate dogs and in 1931 were declared to be a national monument—a Japanese treasure. At that time they were officially designated a pure breed by the mayor of Odate. That city was the capitol of the Akita Prefecture, the northernmost province of the Japanese island of Honshu. Japanese dogs are customarily named for the region in which they prevail, and their original name was Akita Inu (Akita Dog). They were the largest of seven Japanese breeds established in 1931. Akitas' pedigree documentation has been carefully maintained at Odate since that time.

World War II and After

Akita numbers dwindled in Japan during World War II because they were in demand for food and pelts. Others were destroyed to conserve food that was needed for human consumption. Although they neared extinction, a few representatives of the breed somehow survived and began to flourish again in the postwar years of the late 1940s and early 1950s. Akita breeding during that period resulted in the production of two bloodlines, the descendants of which have emigrated to virtually the entire world.

Many American soldiers were so enamored by the sturdiness, loyalty, and beauty of the breed that they acquired Akitas and brought them home. American and allied servicemen are probably responsible for the early popularity of

The Akita of the West is not an exact replica of the Japanese Akita.

Akitas in the United States and other Western countries. During the postwar years of 1945 to 1955 a great number of Akitas were imported into the United States, England, and Canada, and by 1956 a breed club was established in the United States. According to most accounts, the Akita of the Western world has retained the important Japanese Akita characteristics.

Some Well-Known Akitas

No discussion of Akita history is complete without mentioning a few dogs of particular renown. Hachi-Ko was an Akita given to a Tokyo professor in 1924. The professor daily rode a commuter train to and from his suburban home, and his young Akita, Hachi-Ko, accompanied him to the station in the morning and returned to the station to meet him each evening. When Professor Ueno suddenly died of a stroke, Hachi-Ko continued to make his afternoon trip to the train station at the exact hour previously established. After patiently waiting for the train, and finding his master missing, he walked home alone. Although the dog was only about 18 months old when the professor died, Hachi-Ko continued his trip to the station every evening until his own death, nearly 10 years later. A bronze statue of Hachi-Ko stands at Toyko's Shibuya Station today and a ceremony attracts hundreds of dog fanciers to the station to honor Hachi-Ko each year.

United States humanitarian Helen Keller met and fell in love with Akitas during a Japanese speaking tour in 1937. She was presented a puppy, Kamikaze-Go, that she brought home to

New York, but unfortunately it died before one year of age. In 1939 another Akita, Kanzan-Go, was given to her, and it lived as her companion until its death in 1945.

--- **TIP** ---

The Akita Stud Book

Although Akita-type dogs were raised in many Japanese regions, the large northern strains produced in the mountainous Akita Prefecture were undoubtedly the most influential ancestors of today's Akita. In 1927 the Akita Inu Hozankai Society was given the task of recording and maintaining a stud book that documented the parents of every litter produced in Japan. It persists today and helps to preserve the purity of the breed. Every champion Akita is declared a National Art Treasure in Japan.

AKITA DISPOSITION AND TEMPERAMENT

The Akita's courageous personality and loyalty are enhanced by its physical beauty and stature. The pinto Akita has the most striking physical appearance of any dog anywhere. Its rich, thick, deep coat and unusual color patterns are truly outstanding.

Akitas' Unique Features

Colors and Patterns

Akitas are found in a variety of eye-catching colors and patterns. Any color and color combination is acceptable, including pure white, jet black, brindle, and pinto or spotted. Their markings should be brilliant and clear, and never smudged. The pinto's conspicuous snowy white ground color and large, evenly spaced patches of a dark color over the body are outstandingly beautiful.

Conformation

Their conformation is in many ways similar to the sled dogs of Alaska and Siberia. They

A happy puppy may develop an undesirable personality unless it is properly socialized and trained.

were developed under similar conditions, in another frigid part of the world. Their body type is strong and muscular and their coats are similar to other Northern working dogs. As in all purebred dog husbandry, selective breeding has brought about changes in Akitas' physical characteristics from those of the original Japanese animals.

Size

Modern Akitas are larger, more massive animals than they were in the twelfth century. Because of the depletion of the gene pool during World War II, Akitas of today may be traced to a small number of progenitors. Those bred and exhibited in America and Great Britain reflect the postwar development of the breed in the United States. Akitas bred in Japan are usually smaller in stature with lighter bone structure than their Western

Even-tempered with family, the Akita is highly protective when strangers are encountered.

counterparts. Japanese-bred dogs also may have smaller ears, an outstanding coat quality, and sharp, distinct coat color patterns. In Japanese shows, the Akitas are "faced off" with one another, encouraging them to show aggressiveness. The Japanese seem to cultivate and appreciate the aggressive trait in their dogs, and breed to propagate that personality.

It would be a serious judgment error to try to discuss all the characteristics that set Akitas apart from all other breeds but a blunder of equal magnitude would be to neglect to mention a few of those features. The following verbal picture is extracted and paraphrased from the official breed standard, which can be found on the AKC Web page of the Internet, The Akita Club of America Web page, and in printed form in the *AKC Dog Book*.

Description

✔ The male Akitas stand 26 to 28 inches (66 to 71 cm). Their weights, although not mentioned in the official standard, average 95 to 110 pounds (43 to 50 kg) for males and 75 to 90 pounds (34 to 41 kg) for females. Their thick, short necks, dense coats, and bulky bodies give them the appearance of much larger animals. Fanciers state that Akitas are at the lower end of the large breeds, not at the upper end of the

TIP

Names Used in This Book

The author uses the boring and tiresome neutral references to Akitas in a few places. However, writing about real, vital, and interesting dogs should be more personal, so the hero and heroine are given names in various chapters. Spirit is the name of our feminine heroine in some, and in others, Koby is the name of our masculine hero.

middle-sized breeds. When an Akita is seen briefly and by itself, the visual image you receive is that of a huge dog.

✔ Akitas are found in every color and pattern. Virtually all colors are acceptable, including red, silver, fawn, and brindle. The attractive spotted or pinto color patterns are said to be attributable primarily to a postwar dog named Goromaru Go. He was a flashy red and white pinto that indelibly stamped his progeny with those colors and patterns. The breed standards specify that Akita markings should be sharp, distinct, and clear-cut, not smudged or masked.

✔ Akitas' broad, triangular heads also exhibit various colors and patterns. Some dogs have solid-colored heads and others sport dazzling, impressive white masks or blazes, and if equilaterally balanced, they are greatly admired.

✔ Akitas' faces are truly extraordinary. Their expressions are dominated by wide-set, small ears that tip forward, giving the dog an alert or quizzical appearance, even when resting. Their oriental eyes are dark brown, smallish, and almond-shaped.

✔ Although there is a lot of dog between the head and tail, another distinctive feature is the Akita's tail. It is large and full, set high, and carried over the back or against the flank in a three-quarter, full, or double curl that always dips to or below the level of the back. Tail hair is course, straight, without a plume, and is rarely stationary. Akita tails that aren't curled or that are carried away from their backs are considered serious faults.

✔ Akita coats are double, with coarse, dense, plush guard hair, and soft, dense undercoats. Those luxurious coats show no signs of feathering on the legs, which adds to the bulky, sturdy appearance of the entire body.

Akitas' Show History

The Akita Club of America was formed in 1956. The breed was registered in the AKC miscellaneous class in 1972 and was admitted to regular AKC show classification in the Working Group in April, 1973.

Akitas are bred to several standards in different parts of the world, depending on the country where they are produced and shown. Study the applicable breed standard and attend shows and matches to see how the animals are professionally judged and evaluated before you buy an Akita, regardless of the age, sex, or color you choose. Talk to breeders and handlers and ask why a judge placed one dog above another. Familiarize yourself with the major characteristics of the breed. In America, visit the AKC Web site and print a copy of the official standard for your reference. Every Akita standard belabors adjectives such as *large, heavy, broad, firm, wide, deep, strong, thick, muscular, and hard*. Akita temperaments are variously described as *courageous,* dominant, dignified, vigorous, and resilient. Those terms paint a picture of a powerful working dog, one that is aloof and sure of itself.

The Akita Personality, Character, and Behavioral Habits

Some irresponsible backyard Akita breeders may tell prospective puppy buyers that an Akita's personality is wholly hereditary. Others may claim that its personality is totally dependent on its puppyhood environment. Both of those statements are incorrect. Koby's personality (disposition or temperament), is partly inherited from his progenitors and those traits are deeply seated in his brain. However, personality is the product of heredity plus his experiences that happen by chance and those that are purposefully taught from birth throughout his life.

Behavior is the way an individual acts, his comportment, or his social graces. It includes his conduct around other dogs or humans and those traits often can be modified through consistent training. However, each Akita has some definite hereditary tendencies to be aggressive, and those are tougher (or impossible) to change.

A Habit

A *habit* is a tendency to repeated action and a habit can eventually influence many of Koby's personality traits. After a habit has become established, it will be extremely difficult to modify in this strong-willed Akita because if something is done often, it becomes easier to do, and those habits can dominate his whole character. Good habits, ingrained early and regularly, boosted by repeated instruction, are

wonderful. A few bad habits can ruin your relationship with your companion unless you succeed in modifying them.

Character

Koby's character is the sum of the aforementioned qualities and is influenced by his human and animal relationships (socialization). The right time to begin molding his character by gentle treatment and consistent instruction is during the first few weeks of his life. A responsible Akita breeder will begin human socialization before the puppies' eyes open and will continue with that training until the litter is weaned and on the way to new homes. Socialization training should receive high priority from the time Koby enters your door the first time and should continue for the rest of his life.

Note: Akitas are sometimes demanding and have strong territorial-protection instincts that are inherited and can be only partially modified. Akitas belong in a home with a strong leader who will take the family's alpha leader role in the pack from the beginning of the relationship.

Dog-Aggressiveness

Akitas are fierce and dominating when challenged by other dogs and their curiosity and mischievous natures sometimes lead to such challenges. Few if any timid or reclusive Akitas exist. No two Akitas are alike and many are outgoing, fun-loving, and friendly toward other pets that they have known since puppyhood, although that is not always the case. Sometimes Akitas are never trustworthy around other dogs, including those with which they are raised, and they should not be allowed off-leash when any other dogs are in the vicinity. Many Akitas also possess an instinctive predator-prey drive toward small species of animals. Always walk Koby with a chain training collar (or head halter), and a short, stout leash, because total control must be maintained when other animals are met.

Caution: Akitas are strong willed and animal socialization training must be practiced from puppyhood on.

People-Aggressiveness

Some Akitas are also people-aggressive and if that trait begins to form it should be discouraged through gentle, stepwise training. People-socialization training should be continued from the day Koby first enters your home. That socialization should persist while he is still a playful puppy because at that time he trusts everyone he meets in your home. He will become more people-socialized as he meets more people and is petted and considerately handled by those people. Take him on walks around the neighborhood as soon as he is collar- and leash-trained (and vaccinated). Encourage your neighbors and friends to spend a few minutes petting and handling Koby when he is outside of his home environment and invite them to visit him in your house and yard. Everyone will appreciate the time you spend socializing your Akita puppy and his personality will be improved with every agreeable and pleasant human encounter.

To his family Koby may remain docile, an intelligent, lovable, and trainable pet. He might be a bit stubborn and have a mind of his own but is still loving, mannerly, and nonaggressive until a year or more of age. Then around a year of age, his character may change and he may become overly possessive, dominant, and defensive of his family and home.

This Akita puppy radiates a very agreeable disposition.

A friend who is an Akita breeder tells a story about a plumber who came to the house to fix a drain. The plumber went to work under the kitchen sink after he was introduced to one of the family's Akitas, who happened to be in the house at the time. While the friend was busy in another part of the house, the industrious Akita

▬ TIP ▬

Playing with Children

Caution: As a puppy Koby will undoubtedly play with the family children, but all playtimes must be monitored by the adult family members to assure that the play doesn't become too rough.

An Akita youth that appears happy and well socialized.

described as *courageous* or *dignified*. Those terms are a bit esoteric but often are truly applicable.

Akitas and Children

Akitas are affectionate creatures and typically are very gentle with children. They rarely demonstrate short tempers or inappropriate attitudes and actions with their family's children. They are tolerant and many choose to walk away to their crates for a nap when play becomes tiresome. Most Akitas show no aggressiveness toward their family's children even when they are pushed beyond normal limits, but when they wish to be left alone, that decision must be honored by their playmates. Koby will typically guard the family children, and treat other children with deference—provided he receives kind and considerate treatment. His hunting instincts, stamina, and playful disposition make him a wonderful playmate for everyone in his social circle, including children and adults to whom he has been properly introduced.

Children can be vengeful or retaliatory if they are scratched during play and Koby may consider that vindictiveness to be aggression. Hand- or clothes-chewing episodes should be stopped immediately by substituting Koby's toys into the play, but bear in mind that tug toys may lead to aggressiveness and should be avoided. You should personally spend time with all children who come in contact with Koby to assure that proper introductions are made and play rules are clearly understood and closely followed.

quietly picked up each tool in the plumber's bag, one by one, and carried it to the front door. When everything was thus arranged he returned and gently but firmly took the plumber's pants leg, tugged it, and escorted him to the front door. Please note that Akitas commonly carry articles around in their mouths, even wrists and pants legs.

General Qualities

That story is not meant to imply that all Akitas display such cleverness and intelligence. Certainly they don't all fit in any common personality mold, but there are some generalities that apply. Typically, Akitas are bright but reserved. They are happy dogs when in their home environments but they remain possessive wherever they are. As an adult, Koby probably won't act silly or foolish but will not be timid or reclusive. Akitas' temperaments are often

— T I P —

Babies

When Koby is introduced to an infant, the meeting should always be closely monitored and supervised but he should not be put in his crate or another room each time the baby is present because he may learn to resent the infant.

Neighborhood children usually cause no problems with Koby if their presence is continued from his puppyhood and people who are minding their own business are rarely the object of Akita aggression.

Koby has great loyalty and will quickly become territorially aggressive toward strangers who approach his home, regardless of their ages. It doesn't matter if the intruder is a Girl Scout selling cookies or a burly workman coming to repair your dishwasher. If you aren't there to take charge and Koby is guarding the home, he should be crated or confined to another room or to his outdoor kennel.

Confusion and noise: Generally speaking, a household filled with confusion is a poor environment for Koby. That includes screaming children, noisy play, adults going and coming, doors opening and slamming, and the chaos associated with a party in full swing.

Another story comes to mind. An Akita owner's five boys were wrestling on the floor when a neighborhood boy of like age decided to join in the fun. When he piled onto his friends, at their request, the Akita barked loudly, showed his teeth, and ushered the newcomer to the door. The Akita didn't attack the child, didn't touch him in any way, but was content to "herd" the boy from the premises. After the neighbor boy left, the Akita returned to the playroom and continued his vigil—but not all Akitas would be that polite. To prevent confrontations from occurring, the adults of the family should have removed the Akita from the play area when the roughhousing began or prevented the newcomer from joining in until he had been properly introduced to the dog.

A tiny Akita puppy may be apprehensive and intimidated by loud voices and confusion.

Historical Uses of Akitas

Dogfights

Early development of Akitas blended the stubbornness and strong wills of fighting dogs with the scenting ability of sporting dogs. They were used to trail stags, bears, and other game, and some of the earliest reports of Akitas relate to their roles in pit fighting. Although another Japanese breed (the Tosa, or Japanese Mastiff) is better known for its fighting ability, the Akita's prowess in a dogfight is awesome.

That dog-aggressive instinct has not been fully suppressed from Koby's memory bank, and may be expressed in a never-quit attitude. He may demonstrate dominance over other dogs and when allowed, carry that attitude to a physical encounter, a dogfight that should never happen.

Hunting

Akitas are known to "nose out" game and although never having made their mark in America as pointers, setters, or retrievers, in Japan they

TIP

Two Male Akitas

Housing two adult male Akitas together is risky business at best and is never advisable. A male and female, or two females that were spayed before six months of age may live together in harmony, but two males or two intact females will inevitably fight. Once a brawl has ensued, it is unlikely that future peace and compatibility will ever be maintained between the combatants.

TIP

Warning

Your Akita should never be introduced to Schutzhund training, attack training, and defensive or offensive training of any kind! Specialized guard training is a serious mistake that might convert a fine family companion into a monster.

were used to locate and flush ground birds. History relates that they were accomplished and soft-mouthed upland retrievers. Bear hunting was a challenge successfully met with a bow and arrow and a brace of aggressive and fearless Akitas that would keep the bear at bay until killed.

Water Retrieving

Akitas usually are reported to flunk the test for water retrievers because of the character of their heavy double coats that absorb great amounts of water. Their swimming abilities can't compare to the specialized hunting breeds of today, including spaniels, Labradors, Chesapeakes, and other water retrievers. In spite of that limitation, reports exist of Akitas that were trained by fishermen to herd fish into their nets by swimming around them—an enviable feat at the very least!

Herding

Akitas apparently were used as herding dogs in the seventeenth century in the mountainous, northern regions of Honshu. The cold, snowy, northwest Sea of Japan environment no doubt exerted strong influence on the dog's robust stamina, solid bone structure, and dense coats. Like other Northern dogs of today, they retain

A stately pinto Akita that is always on duty in his backyard or in the house.

much of the toughness related to the environment of their origin.

Sledding, Packing, and Police Work

Akitas have proven themselves in weight-pulling contests on the ice and are in their element when hitched to a sled. However, it is rare to find Akitas used in today's sled teams that are made up of Alaskan Malamutes, Siberian Huskies, Samoyeds, and other Northern breeds. The reason may be associated with the Akita propensity to dominate all other dogs in its society.

Akitas are frequently used to carry backpacks, and sometimes are hitched to carts. Occasion-ally they are reported to be used in police work but that rarely is a suitable vocation for them because of their natural aggressiveness, and when combined with police training, their natural aggressiveness might overflow and become dangerous.

Security, Watch-, or Guard Dog

Akitas are strong-willed dogs that have a wired-in territorial protective instinct that is not likely to be suppressed. All dogs have the ability to read unexpected human situations, probably by means of detection and evaluation of certain pheromones, which are types of scent that are

This mature Akita pet is very possessive of his territory.

emitted by humans and other animals. Pheromone release is detected especially when a person is stricken with fear, startled, suddenly challenged, or panicky. When Koby senses fear or discomfort in his human companion, he goes into a protective mode even if no verbal alarm, gestures, or physical actions are evident. A dominant Akita in a protective mode is not apt to back down from anyone or anything. The solid, tough, and determined Akita is an excellent guard dog and a formidable, living security system in your home. Although Koby is a peace-loving, well-socialized, gentle pet, he will meet any challenge he perceives.

Akitas are easily overtrained and they take their training to heart, which ruins them for-

ever as family pets. In contemporary American society, attack dogs or fighting dogs aren't tolerated. Your household liability insurance premium will probably increase or the company might even cancel the policy if you enroll Koby in guard training of any nature.

Akitas have innate defensive ideas of their own. A friend relates a story about her Akita's natural protective instincts. When taking a walk one morning, she realized her Akita that was walking at heel on her left side, was pushing her off the sidewalk each time a stranger was met on the street. The dog leaned into her and gradually exerted pressure on her left leg, pushing her to one side and assuring that a wide berth was established between the stranger and his mistress. Guarding, defensive action, and protectiveness are inherent in all Akitas.

The Akita's Value as a Pet

Koby will make a wonderful, winsome pet. Give him a loving and caring home and family to look after and he will be a fine companion.

The laughing Akita can be very serious when sensing danger.

═══ CHECKLIST ═══

Characteristics

Koby will respond to affection, kindness, and gentleness, and will develop the following characteristics:

✔ *Quietness.* He will very likely be unobtrusive, a bit lazy, and will enjoy human interaction. Akitas hardly ever bark.

✔ *Exercise.* Koby won't require an abundance of physical exercise and will accept apartment living if he is given regular walks. He will love a fenced yard when it is available.

✔ *Play.* He will love his family and its children but playing with small children requires ongoing monitoring and socializing (see page 13).

✔ *Obedience.* Koby will thrive on training because it is an extension of bonding. However, he will get bored rather quickly and might demonstrate a stubborn streak. That inclination can be detoured with short and varied training sessions, gentleness, and love.

Adoption of an Adult Akita

Be very wary of taking the responsibility of an older Akita unless you have a complete, accurate account of its nature. Note that an adult Akita's physical beauty is not indicative of its past training, its attitude, or its life experiences. Generally, Akita rescue organizations place very few of their dogs into family homes because adult rescued Akitas' history and background are spotty at best. If you have children, be doubly careful because an Akita that comes with incomplete or inaccurate past history might be the proverbial loose cannon on deck and you can't afford the risk.

CHOOSING YOUR AKITA PUPPY

A new Akita puppy is a major investment of your time and money. Of vital concern are the immediate needs of the Akita puppy, but equally important are her future needs, after she has reached maturity. Spirit will share your home for the next dozen years and she deserves planning that befits the nature and needs as an adult.

Timing

A poor time to shop for any pet is near the holidays or shortly before you leave on vacation. Try to choose a convenient season, one that will allow you to devote a significant amount of quality time with the new family member. Select a week when you have few visitors and when the family routine is quiet and stable. Don't introduce Spirit into confusion and chaos. Bonding, socialization training, and house-training are all adjustments to a new environment that is a challenge for Spirit under ideal circumstances.

Note: Reconsider any thoughts you might have about buying an Akita as a surprise gift for anyone. Gifts are usually appreciated except when the gift happens to be a living, loving,

An Akita puppy must be carefully chosen after many factors are considered.

responsibility, in which case the gift might be remembered for all the wrong reasons.

The Truth About Gifts

✔ Unless the receiver is fully in accord with your plans and the timing is perfect, don't do it.
✔ Impulse buying is a pitfall that can lead to heartache.
✔ Don't buy an Akita for a child who is too young to care for it properly, or for one who has no interest in owning a pet.
✔ A family companion should be discussed at length with everyone concerned with its care, feeding, and training.
✔ Ground rules should be decided upon before even looking for an Akita puppy.
✔ Your family's financial and emotional limitations must be considered.
✔ The drain on your personal time should be considered.

Wait a year or two if you haven't the necessary time to devote to the puppy's care, training, feeding, and preventive health duties.

What to Look For

It is difficult to look at a six-week-old puppy and visualize her as an adult. For that reason, it is important to see Spirit's parents and, if possible, some of their adult offspring from previous litters. When you first see a litter of cuddly little Akita puppies, you will appreciate the difficulty of comparing them to 100-pound (45-kg) adults that you have seen winning the purple and blue show ribbons. Be aware of the following:

✔ Spirit's small ears are folded down until about 9 to 14 weeks of age, and if they aren't standing up by 16 weeks of age, taping is required.

✔ Her tail will begin to curl when she is about four weeks old, and by eight weeks the typical Akita tail should be apparent. If it is not well curled by three to four months of age, it will probably remain uncurled throughout her life.

✔ A young Akita puppy doesn't have a typical broad, flat forehead. That feature usually develops over several years and sometimes has not reached its final shape until two to five years of age.

✔ Spirit will reach her maximum height by 18 months or two years of age, and her body will continue to fill out until she is about five years of age.

✔ Her scissors bite should be apparent at an early age and that feature is very important to check for when she is purchased. A scissors bite means the upper incisors (front teeth) are positioned just in front of, and touching, the lower incisors.

✔ Angulation of Spirit's leg joints, her body length, feet and hock positioning, and pastern strength may be unapparent to you but those features are quickly recognized by experts, which makes it even more important to see her parents and adult offspring of her parents.

Prepurchase Considerations

✔ Adequate exercise is required by all puppies. Your home should have an ample, tightly fenced yard. Or, if you live in an apartment, Spirit will need several daily walks.

✔ Traveling sometimes presents problems for inexperienced owners. If you vacation, will you board Spirit in a kennel or take her with you? How will she travel, in her kennel in the car, or in a special harness that fastens onto the seat belt?

✔ Are sufficient funds available for regular vaccinations and others that might be needed when traveling?

✔ Are you able to buy the best dog food available, as well as treats and chew toys?

✔ Can you take the time required for Spirit's training? Will you train and socialize her with people and dogs? Can you afford the necessary equipment such as collars, leashes, and in some cases, a professional training consultant's fee?

All of those questions must be answered in the affirmative before beginning the actual

An Akita that has discovered the wild outdoors.

search for an Akita puppy. If you are thinking puppy, use intelligent reasoning and not your emotions. Don't buy an Akita because it is cute and cuddly. If you don't have the space and money for a large breed and you don't have time to set aside for an Akita, perhaps you should be looking for a gerbil or goldfish.

Note: If the dominant personality of an Akita doesn't appeal to you, use your head, change your mind, and look for a more appropriate breed.

An Akita is not the best pet for everyone. Akita ownership carries with it responsibilities that aren't quite as important when considering a smaller, less aggressive breed. However, if you have chosen an Akita from the several hundred pure breeds that exist worldwide (more than 150 registered by AKC alone), you will enjoy your choice and you will be in good company. In 2005 Akitas ranked 51 in the AKC registry with 2,329 total registered.

Quality

For the purposes of this discussion, Spirit's *quality* doesn't refer to her health or her merit as a pet. The term is used to designate her showing and breeding potential. The designations used here include *show quality, breeding quality*, and *pet quality.*

Show Quality

Show-quality Akitas are those that meet the breed standard in nearly all categories, the Akitas that bring home the ribbons and trophies from dog shows.

Note: Very few show-quality puppies are produced in a litter even when both parents are winners.

An experienced breeder might choose one or two puppies from a litter to reserve for potential showing. Choosing show-quality puppies is an inexact science that requires expertise and ability and develops only with extensive experience and knowledge of the breed. Some Akita breeders can pick a show-quality puppy out of a litter at six or eight weeks of age but that talent is not easily obtained and comes only after raising and showing many candidates from dozens of litters.

The reservoir of show-quality puppies is quite small in any breed, because no one can produce a *perfect* dog. Often the best puppies, the ones that approach the breed standard, are retained by the breeder and sold only if they mature to be less perfect than formerly believed.

Note: Show-quality puppies command higher prices than pet-quality puppies because of their rarity.

Ethical breeders will usually be reticent to designate a weanling Akita as show quality. Only after a certain amount of growth and development is there any degree of certainty that the puppy is nearing perfection, and likely to be a winner. Even then, breeders and buyers alike are regularly fooled.

Show dogs might be considered the cream of the Akita crop. For a potential buyer, a show-quality puppy constitutes a considerable investment that is justified only if you intend to exhibit Spirit. If you are considering showing, discuss co-ownership or *Limited Registration* with the breeder, in which case, Spirit is yours, but if you decide to breed her, you must do so with the breeder's consent and cooperation. However, if show dogs are not your cup of tea, you can acquire a beautiful Akita companion pet that won't stretch your budget quite so far.

Breeding Quality

Very few Akita puppies possess the perfection of form and function needed to clear all the health hurdles, win in shows, and produce a litter of truly extraordinary puppies. If you are thinking about breeding Spirit at some time in the future, you should shop for the best show-quality puppy you can find and be prepared to spend endless hours and a great deal of money to raise her, train her, travel to shows with her, and perhaps hire a professional handler to show her.

> If show dogs are the cream of the crop, breeding-quality Akitas are the cream of the show dogs.

A female Akita must be more than two years old before she can be considered for breeding. Only after she has reached that age can she undergo the necessary hereditary disease testing. By then she will have been matched against

This well-behaved adult is right at home on his acreage.

her peers in enough shows to prove her conformational perfection, and her disposition will have proven stable. However, even if you fork out the money for a breeding-quality female, don't count her puppies before they are born.

Akita breeding is a wonderful hobby and should be pursued only by those who are willing and can afford to spend the time and money to do it right! For this reason, most Akita fanciers turn from the show and breeding-quality puppies to pet-quality companions.

Pet Quality

Conscientious Akita breeders do not have some females that produce *pets* and others that produce *show-quality* puppies. Hereditary faults

are not found in pet-quality puppies to any greater or lesser degree than in show-quality puppies. Pet quality is the category that receives most of the attention in this manual. Akita admirers are captivated by the Akitas' unique

TIP

Pet Akitas

Pet Akitas are likely to have more minor visible faults than their more pricy siblings but those conformational faults do not denigrate the value of a companion pet.

This sturdy male Akita manifests a strong, possessive temperament.

appearance and fascinated with their personalities. That infatuation is enhanced by the Akita temperament, physical soundness, and agility—because the average pet owner wants an Akita as a friend, companion, and playmate. They want a beautiful pet, one that is easily recognized as a fine purebred Akita. Owners may feed their egos with framed registration certificates and may even rave to friends about the number of AKC champions in their pet's pedigree, but few are interested in showing and breeding their pets. That is a healthy situation because very few Akitas should be shown or bred.

Pet-quality Akitas possess the same personalities, colors, coats, and general conformation as their higher-priced siblings—they just don't measure up to the breed standard quite so well. A companion's personality, strength, agility, and trainability should not differ from those higher priced puppies.

There is another advantage to buying a pet Akita besides its price. Often, breeders will part with a pet from a litter at an earlier age than those they expect to be show dogs. It is not a good idea to take puppies from their nest before six weeks of age but we certainly miss a lot of fun when we acquire a puppy after it is several months old.

Linebreeding

How can you be sure Spirit, a pet-quality puppy, is not going to develop a hereditary problem? You can't, or at least you can't be positive, but the odds will be in your favor if you buy from an ethical, responsible Akita breeder. The best course for an ethical breeder to take is to have their brood stock examined and certified by experts, and use that gene pool without exception. Linebreeding is a technique wherein a female Akita is bred to a distant relative. That is an acceptable technique when carefully used and when all breeding animals are chosen from certified-clean stock. It becomes dangerous when done without consideration of minor weaknesses of the individuals being bred. Linebreeding can improve a breed and help to eliminate hereditary diseases but it can also be disastrous when tried by amateur breeders.

The Downside of Akitas

Consider these points before you buy:
✔ Akitas are ambitious dogs that thrive on regular exercise.

✔ They are strong-willed dogs that require early and continual socialization with humans and other dogs.

✔ They need human leadership and control as they are often dog-aggressive and human-aggressive, even if you supply extensive dominance (leadership) training.

✔ They are not likely to accept the dominance of other household pets.

✔ If your personality tends to be permissive, and if you often yield to the demands of others, an Akita is not the breed for you.

Which Sex to Choose

If you are unsure whether or not you might eventually want to show and breed your Akita, your choice between a male or female is of utmost importance because only intact males and females can be shown. Most pets are spayed or castrated before maturity and the sex of a companion is somewhat irrelevant.

The proper time for spaying your female or castrating your male Akita depends on many factors. Females can, and often should be spayed soon after they finish their puppyhood vaccinations, and males can be castrated at the same age. The safety of neutering males and spaying females at a young age has been proven to nearly everyone's satisfaction and many shelters routinely practice that program. Three-month-old puppies recover quickly from general anesthesia and have no measurable problems associated with the surgery. The mortality rate is almost nonexistent in males and females that are neutered and spayed at early ages.

Another argument for spaying young puppies is that an older bitch may have more fat deposits on the organs removed and that can increase the surgical risk and may require a longer period of anesthesia. (See discussion on spaying and castrating on page 79.)

Most canine companions are what we make of them. Akitas of either sex will remember their puppyhood treatment. If owners were rough with them, they will never be as gentle and loving as they might have been if they had received more consideration when puppies. If you are kind to Spirit when she is a puppy, she will reflect that love and gentleness when grown. If you spend time with her when she is a few months old, she will respond accordingly.

Note: Pet ownership requires patience, consideration, and kindness throughout life.

Breeders

Professional Akita Breeders

Professional, reputable Akita breeders are the best sources for your new puppy. They can be located by attending a dog show in your area and meeting them in person. Akita shows are advertised in *Akita World* magazine and all-breed shows are advertised in the *AKC Gazette* or *Dog World* magazine.

Warning: Don't buy your Akita puppy until you talk, in person, to the individual who has raised it, discuss the puppy's pedigree, personality, and nutrition, and personally go to see it, handle the puppy as well as the puppy's siblings and dam.

Finding a Breeder

✔ To find a reputable Akita breeder, visit the AKC Web site, click on *Akitas*, then *Akita Club of America*. You will find the e-mail address or telephone number of the secretary of the

Tug toys can create an overly competitive personality that may backfire later.

Akita Club who will furnish breeder referrals in your area.

✔ Make telephone contact with a few breeders and set up a meeting with them.

✔ Go to the breeders' homes and talk to each one. Ask them questions and expect to be quizzed in return.

✔ If a breeder has a litter of puppies that can be shown to you, by all means check them out.

✔ Evaluate the facility's cleanliness, the temperaments of the dogs you meet, and the evidence of dog show wins standing on the mantle and hanging from every wall. Notice the pictures of fine Akitas and ask about them.

Most breeders are Akita fanciers who show a couple of dogs and have one or two bitches that are bred every year or two. A few of the breeders may have a stud dog, and most have a show-potential, half-grown puppy, and maybe a retired bitch or two. It is rarely a big business. Breeding dogs, even beautiful Akitas, is not a particularly lucrative vocation. Reputable Akita breeders have one thing in common—they are dedicated to Akitas and their motivation is to improve the breed with each breeding.

Newspaper ads are another source—but be wary of charlatans! Sometimes owners will advertise their Akita for sale because, for some reason, they must part with their pet. Maybe they have lost a spouse, or must downsize, or are moving from the area and can't take their big dog along. Maybe they don't have time to train or socialize their Akita and are willing to re-home their pet instead of neglecting it. If you find such an Akita, visit its home, ask to see its registration papers, ask its breeder's name, pet and handle it, and if all looks well, leave a deposit and take the dog to your veterinarian for a professional consultation. Contact the puppy's breeder, discuss the situation, and follow the advice you have obtained from those professionals.

Backyard Breeders

These imposters often advertise in newspapers, but be aware that a backyard breeder will often have much less intimate knowledge of the Akita breed than a professional. That person probably bought an Akita puppy from another backyard breeder, paid an enormous price, and when the puppy came into heat, decided to recoup the investment by breeding her. The seller may have the proper AKC registration papers on the puppy because the AKC is not a regulatory agency and will register any litter that is born to an AKC-registered dam and sired by a registered male.

Some newspaper ads state that a litter of Akita puppies is not registered but its parents are purebred. At least some weanling puppies of a litter born to a purebred Akita dam may resemble their mother. However, if you can't see the sire and it was a mixed breed, a puppy might grow into an adult that resembles no particular breed. Buying an Akita puppy from a backyard breeder is fraught with inherent problems!

Pet Shops

Those impulse-buyer stores are often very clean, well appointed, attractive, and well staffed by polite and knowledgeable young clerks. It is fun to visit a pet shop because they display healthy-appearing, energetic, and amusing puppies that catch your eye with their

rough-and-tumble play. Pet shops thrive in a heavy-traffic mall because dog lovers can't keep their hands off the clean, cute, well-groomed, and cuddly puppies. However, if you are seriously considering buying your Akita in a pet shop, make certain that you glean any information that you can about the puppy's background. Pet shops are usually the "middle man" in the transaction, the puppies having been born and raised elsewhere. The puppy will come with an AKC registration form properly completed by the seller, but probably not a pedigree. It will have a short-term, limited, health guarantee, vaccination, and worming records, but your knowledge of its parents is zero.

Thus, although the quickest way to find an Akita may be through a newspaper ad or a reputable pet shop, your chance of getting a puppy that has the best parentage, health care, and early experiences is best if you find a reputable, knowledgeable breeder.

Personality Prediction

Spirit's adult personality is somewhat unpredictable when she is six or seven weeks old because temperaments are partly developmental (a product of environment and experience), and partly inherited. Spirit's personality is not cast in stone at the time of birth but certain traits can be found early in life. If you are shopping for a recently weaned Akita, try to select a puppy that is somewhat independent, curious, and playful. If all puppies in the litter are sleeping in a heap, and when you wake them they quickly hurry to the warmth and security of their dam, they are too young to take from her. However, if they tug at toys, romp about, and show more interest than apprehension when you approach, they are probably about ready for new homes.

Warning: Don't choose an Akita puppy because of its outstanding physical beauty if it displays aggressive tendencies or timidity.

If a puppy hides from you and shies from your hand, it is either too young to take from its nest or is slow to socialize. Wait a week and visit again.

Tests

Toss a wad of paper across the room and if one puppy chases it and attempts to play with the paper, make note of that puppy. Put a couple of marbles into an empty soda can and tape over the hole. Roll the can slowly across the floor and check the reaction of the puppies. If most of them run and hide but one puppy is startled for a second, then slowly approaches the can to investigate, make note of that puppy.

As a final test, cradle the curious puppy upside down in your arms for a few minutes. If she is content to lie there quietly while you pet and reassure her, she is probably ready to socialize and should make a good pet. If she struggles and continually tries to escape, better try another puppy or delay your selection for a week or two. If you set her down near her siblings and she climbs back on your lap and licks your chin, she is a most promising candidate. If you stand to leave and she follows you to the door, it is probably a match.

Meet the Parents

Before choosing a puppy you should be introduced to its parents or at least to its dam. Spend some time with them and any other close relatives that are available. Handle them, pet them, and make friends. If either parent shows timidity, fear, or overt aggressiveness, you should be looking elsewhere for your new companion. After being around the Akita dam for an hour, if you are not comfortable with her, you probably won't be comfortable with one of her puppies.

The dam will be protective of her puppies but after she is called from her brood and is introduced formally to the visitors, she should calm down and proudly show her family to you. She will probably look a bit drawn and saggy at weaning time because the nutritional drain associated with lactation (supplying milk for a litter of hungry Akita puppies), is significant. Her coat will be a bit dryer than usual and she will be thinner than she was before being bred. That is normal and shouldn't alarm you.

This Akita puppy is cautiously friendly toward his visitor.

Puppy Health Status

Perfect conformation is rarely attainable in any dog, regardless of its age or breed. It is likely that some minor fault in its physical makeup, markings, or carriage will be found. Likewise, personalities or habits often need some adjustments to attune them to their new owners. Those imperfections can be accepted and corrected but good health is not a negotiable commodity.

Signs of Poor Health

When you visit a breeder to look at puppies, pay particular attention to the general appearance of all of the dogs present.

Veterinary Charts

When puppies are weaned and ready for new homes, they are usually examined by the breeder's veterinarian who should make charts for each puppy, which should specify

• Examination date and the name of the person who performed the exam.

• Examination results, including any abnormalities found.

• The vaccinations administered, which includes the name of the product used and the diseases for which vaccinated. If vaccines were given by the breeder, ask to see the label from the vaccine and copy off the product's name and diseases covered.

• The scheduled date for revaccination.

• The results of fecal examinations and the dose and name of the worm medication given if the exam was positive.

CHECKLIST

Health Checks

✔ If any puppies or adults are coughing or sneezing, beware.

✔ If evidence of diarrhea or vomiting is seen in the kennel area, good health is suspect.

✔ If puppies have feces on their tails or hind legs, delay your purchase.

✔ If any puppies have yellow, mucoid ocular or nasal discharge, their health is not normal.

✔ If puppies are thin, pot-bellied, inactive, lethargic, or act drowsy, illnesses may be present.

✔ Good appetite. Healthy Akita puppies are always ready to eat. If you see a litter at feeding time you will witness healthy puppies attacking their food with enthusiasm.

✔ Bright eyes with no cloudiness or discharge.

✔ A moist, dark nose pad with no discharge or lack of pigmentation.

✔ Bright pink oral mucous membranes, including tongue, gums, and inside of lips.

✔ Shiny, clean coat without evidence of feces on the tail or hair around the anus.

✔ A supple skin that pops back to its normal position after a fold is gently pinched up over the withers.

✔ No skin lesions such as hairless spots or redness of the skin.

✔ Head and tail held up in normal Akita style.

✔ An energetic tongue on one end of the puppy and an animated tail on the other.

• The date another fecal exam or worm treatment should be scheduled.

Never agree to take a puppy home if it "isn't feeling well," with the seller's promise that if it is not better tomorrow, you can return it. If you are suspicious about the health of your prospective Akita, wait a week and revisit or find another source.

Important: Once you accept responsibility for the life and care of a pet, you must do whatever is necessary to maintain good health for the rest of the Akita's life, but in the beginning, you are entitled to a puppy in perfect health.

A Healthy Puppy

Signs of a healthy puppy include

✔ Curiosity. An investigative trait is the mark of a good, healthy Akita puppy.

✔ Active, robust play with its siblings. A shy or reticent puppy is a sign of poor health or personality fault.

Breeder's Guarantee

You should receive the original document, which should contain a number of items:

• A statement that the present health of the puppy is normal.

• A statement that the puppy must be taken to a qualified veterinarian for examination within two days (48 hours) from the time of purchase.

• A very progressive breeder *may* guarantee that Spirit will place well in dog shows and if she is properly trained and handled. If the puppy doesn't meet that expectation, the breeder may offer to replace your puppy with another at a reduced price.

• A promise to take the puppy back if a veterinary examination within 48 hours of purchase

reveals any health problem, and if the puppy is returned to the breeder within 24 hours of the time of the professional health exam.

• A promise to take the puppy back if it doesn't work out in your home. A portion of the purchase price will be refunded to the buyer, the amount to be determined by the date and the condition of the puppy when returned, and if the puppy is in good health, which will be ascertained by a veterinary examination.

A disclaimer might be added, which states that you receive no refund after the puppy has lived for an extended time in your home and has had no training or socialization. Likewise, you can't expect a refund if the puppy is returned in poor nutritional status or with evidence of abuse.

A guarantee doesn't cover Spirit's abilities, intelligence, attitude, personality, future health, or any other intangible or vague reason for your desire to sever your relationship with the Akita.

A breeder's guarantee might only mean that if you aren't able to cope with Spirit for any reason, she won't go to a shelter. It is no sin to find yourself in a situation in which you cannot keep your Akita—but it is unconscionable to deny your stewardship responsibility and dump Spirit in a dog pound or shelter. Akitas deserve

A bright and alert Akita is ready for a romp.

better treatment. If you do not receive a "take back" guarantee and you must re-home your Akita, please call another breeder and describe the situation. That person may know of a rescue organization that will help you.

Your Decision Is Made!

Leave a deposit with the breeder and take Spirit to your veterinarian for a prepurchase exam (see Health Chapter, page 65). After the physical examination, if the clinician finds no alarming deviations from normal, and pronounces your new puppy healthy, finish your negotiations with the breeder, pack up the following items, and take your new Akita puppy home.

Curiosity and ambition are excellent traits for an Akita puppy to display.

Sales Documents

✔ A signed and dated receipt for your payment.
✔ All agreements you have made relative to neutering or breeding the puppy.
✔ An AKC registration form or limited registration papers.
✔ A signed and dated guarantee if one is agreed upon.
✔ Diet description that specifies the food being fed, and Spirit's future feeding schedule.
✔ A copy of the veterinary examination, worming, and vaccination certificates with the appropriate dates, by whom administered, and dates when additional treatments are due.

In addition to those documents, the breeder should furnish you a few days' supply of the food that has been fed to Spirit. Buy the same product and continue to feed it for a week or two, even if your intention is to change to another food later. Puppy environmental changes will be traumatic enough without dietary changes added to them.

Obtaining an Older Dog

Nobody wants to begin an Akita relationship with a senile companion, but sometimes the best choice is an Akita between six months and two or three years old—if an accurate past history is known, the dog is healthy, has a reliable disposition, and you have return privileges.

Advantages of an Adult

✔ Puppyhood vaccinations are finished and you can concentrate on boosters and preventive parasite control. In other words, you face a reduced financial obligation.
✔ Socialization is already well underway.
✔ House-training and basic obedience training are established and hopefully the candidate has been taught some good manners.
✔ Its social habits and disposition are well established and can be evaluated.
✔ Spaying or castration has been done and the fee has been absorbed by the former owner.
✔ Focus is established quicker in a mature dog and that may be advantageous in training.
✔ Bonding is slower in an older dog but once a reciprocal friendship, confidence, and trust are established, the bond may be stronger than you expected.

Downside of an Adult

✔ You are taking someone's word about the dog's personality and past history.

✔ Puppies bond quickly; an older dog will bond with its family but it takes longer.

✔ Dogs are followers and your rules and habits must be taught to a less receptive canine mind.

✔ Teaching an older dog to abide by your training methods will require more rewards and gentle, consistent training.

✔ An adult Akita will be slower than a new puppy to accept your home, family, and lifestyle.

Advertising: Perhaps you can advertise in Akita newsletters or on the verbal grapevine for a young adult Akita that needs a new home. Sometimes, reputable Akita breeders will have a young adult that was kept for a number of months to discover its show potential and if that possibility didn't materialize, the youngster that didn't quite measure up may be available.

Other breeders: Other breeders may have taken an Akita youth back because the buyer couldn't keep it, or an older adult that has been retired from the show ring or breeding program may be available. No matter where you find your adult Akita, you must remember that an adult adapts slowly, requires loads of love and attention, and gentle care when handling. Its habits can be modified but those changes should not be pressed. An adult Akita is likely to be stubborn, and mutual trust and respect must be established before intensive training can begin. The way to establish that trust is to spend a great deal of time with your companion. A walk in the woods every day will allow each member of the team to learn about the other and even a half hour of playtime in the backyard will help.

This sturdy male displays many of the adult Akita's typical physical characteristics.

TIP

Adult Akitas

When you have a family with young children, adoption of an adult Akita may be taking an unreasonable chance. If you decide to try adult adoption, contact the Akita Club of America secretary and obtain the names of Akita rescue organizations to help you. Most rescue organizations insist on performing a psychological profile on their adult dogs before they are re-homed.

BRINGING YOUR AKITA PUPPY HOME

Akitas' size, strength, coat, and ancestry certainly suggest that they are bred to be housed in outside kennels. However, Koby will be a happier companion if he spends a significant time inside your home and sleeps beside your bed. Akitas can tolerate outdoor kennel housing in mild climates but they thrive when allowed to be near their families.

Handling Your Akita

When Koby comes home don't allow him to be mauled and passed like a beach ball from one person to another. Handle him gently and let him wander at your feet from one place to another. From the beginning, it is important to treat Koby in the same manner that he will be treated as an adult. If he is to be a companion, he needs to be treated as such. Allow him to join your activities because he prefers to be present at family functions. If he is confined to a pen and isolated from the family, away from the action, or put outside when the family is inside, he may become destructive. Bad habits will begin, like digging, chewing shrubs, and generally being a nuisance.

A quizzical expression on a curious Akita puppy, trying to decide its next move.

Socialization

Socialization begins within your family. Everyone in the family should pet, cuddle, and play with little Koby. After he has had his puppyhood vaccinations, that social circle should be expanded to include neighbors, children and adults alike. Carry or lead him to the mailbox and introduce him to the mail carrier. Let him accompany you to the door to receive packages from delivery persons. After his puppyhood vaccinations, take him for walks on a leash when children are rollerblading or riding bicycles, and when they stop to pet him, introduce him properly and tell them that he appreciates gentle hands, just like they do.

A Puppy in the House

Even if you have a backyard fence and lawn, remember that he is your companion and will

An Akita puppy is a bundle of energy that needs direction.

appreciate being where people are most of the time; however, your home will need attention to protect him from injury. Before Koby is allowed in your home you should thoroughly inspect and puppy-proof every room to which he will have access.

Urgent! *Keep these numbers handy: National Poison Center Telephone 800-548-2423 or 900-680-0000. ASPCA Poison Center 888-426-4435.*

Eventually, Koby will become a trusted housemate but it is best to never allow a young Akita puppy to be in any room without the supervision of at least one adult member of the family.

Hazards

✔ Telephone, computer, and appliance cords that hang over the edge of cabinet tops should be tied up. Unplug electrical cords of all types because dangling cords become playthings for a curious Akita. Even those that are unplugged can wrap around Koby's neck and when wires are chewed, gastrointestinal problems may follow.

✔ An energetic Koby may attack draperies and curtains that swing within his reach.

✔ Secure cupboard doors because many household chemicals are toxic, and even harmless products make a horrible mess for you to clean up.

✔ Plastic and steel wool scrubbers are delightful to chew but the fine steel wires or abrasive plastic strands can cause major gastric upsets that may require medical attention.

✔ When synthetic or natural sponges are swallowed, they swell up, obstruct the intestinal passageway, and often require surgical removal.

✔ Philodendron, poinsettia, and a variety of other household plants are toxic and all plants make dangerous chew toys for your Akita puppy. If a plant is attacked, it will undoubtedly end up on the floor among damp potting soil, shreds of leaves, and general mess, so *keep all household plants well out of your Akita puppy's reach!*

✔ Artificial foliage and silk plants are dangerous because most stems are made of wire that can entangle on tiny teeth, lacerate tender gums, or cause serious damage to Koby's intestinal tract.

✔ Bookshelves and the books on them are at risk. A nice leather cover is a joy to chew up but a first edition might be hard to replace.

✔ Wastebaskets and their contents are especially attractive because paper wads, paper

Remember that cuteness is transient but a well-socialized Akita lasts forever.

clips, staples, and rubber bands can be particularly dangerous.

✔ Children play on the floor, have toys lying on beds, dolls on low shelves, and gobs of clay on little tables. Koby is a clever but sneaky puppy and he can grab a wad of clay and have it chewed and swallowed before the child realizes what has happened. Keep all children's room doors tightly closed, whether or not the kids are playing there.

✔ Tablecloths, doilies, and table scarves that hang over the edge make great tug toys for Koby.

✔ Throw rugs and small pillows, especially those with tassels, may provide your Akita puppy with a few minutes of fun, but the articles will suffer from the encounter.

Note: A puppy's attraction to an article is directly proportional to its replacement cost. For some unknown reason, an old worn-out shoe isn't nearly as attractive as a new one just purchased for a party. Koby will find your child's most revered doll or your most expensive gloves.

A Practical Solution

Koby wants to spend much of his waking days with you. While he is still a puppy, teach him what is his and what is not. Install puppy gates on doorways to keep him from restricted areas but don't use the collapsing or folding child-proof gates because their V-type accordion-construction may trap his head and neck.

If none of the preceding suggestions are viable in your household, a portable, collapsible, X-Pen can be purchased in a pet supply store.

Such a pen will allow Koby to keep you in sight while he chews his favorite nylon bone, gets a drink anytime, and sleeps on his mat.

Crating for certain purposes and for limited times is another solution. Crate confinement should never be regarded by Koby as punishment and the same conditions apply as are discussed in the house-training discussion on pages 50 to 52.

A Puppy in the Yard

✔ Police the backyard, putting away every item that can be considered dangerous before Koby arrives in your home.

✔ Chain-link fences are preferable to wooden ones for obvious reasons.

✔ Adjust or repair fences if they don't reach to the ground to discourage Koby's digging propensity.

These Akitas are quite well adjusted to one another.

✔ Garden hoses should be kept in the garage or hung out of his reach.

✔ All chemicals should be locked up or put on high shelves in the shed or garage. If Koby chews on a container and swallows even a small amount of garden chemical insecticides, he could be in big trouble.

✔ Fertilizers that are applied to the lawn should be watered well into the soil and all puddles dried up before Koby is allowed access to the yard because if he drinks from them or steps in the chemical solution and licks his feet, poisoning may result.

✔ If Koby chews the package from the fertilizer, call your veterinarian immediately. Read the label to the clinician and follow the directions given. Don't attempt to treat your pet unless no professional help can be contacted. If you must treat, follow the directions on the package or those of the Poison Control office. A puppy's

heart and respiratory rates are rapid, and if his stomach is empty, the product will be quickly absorbed and even a small amount of a toxic substance can be quite dangerous.

✔ Some antifreeze has a sweet taste that dogs usually like. It contains a kidney toxin that can kill your dog and unfortunately, treatment is not very effective, even when the poisoning is discovered early. Therefore, *keep all antifreeze out of the reach of dogs!* If antifreeze poisoning is suspected, obtain professional help immediately.

✔ Don't leave oils, greases, or other automobile products where Koby can reach them.

✔ Paint, turpentine, paint thinner, and acetone should be stored on high shelves. Paint removers are particularly dangerous and even a quick investigative lick can cause severe tongue burns. A clumsy puppy might tip over a can and find his feet bathed in the caustic fluid. If that happens, rinse off the feet immediately with copious

Physical beauty is not the only trait to look for in an Akita.

quantities of cool water. Then wash his feet with soap and water and notify your veterinarian.

✔ Swimming pools can be a threat to Koby's life. All dogs can swim but most pools are not equipped with escape ladders that can be used by dogs. If you have a backyard pool, buy or construct a ramp or steps to assure Koby's safe escape and teach him to use those means to emerge from the pool.

If the foregoing discussion leaves you with the impression that Akita puppies are animated, relentless, destructive forces, please understand that those are worst-case scenarios. Akita puppies are no more mischievous than any other puppies, and are not bent on destruction. By identifying hazards, you might save your puppy's life, or you may at least save yourself some money.

LIFE WITH AN AKITA PUPPY

Most new owners joyfully anticipate sharing their lives with their new housemates, but for the first few months, puppies require a great deal of personal attention that should not be delegated to your children or spouse.

Necessary Equipment

Go to a pet supply store and purchase the following gear. You will need other items later but for now these articles will suffice.

✔ A small web or leather collar that is fitted so that two fingers can slip between the collar and Spirit's neck.

✔ A 4-foot-long (1.2-m) web or leather leash.

✔ A metal identification tag with your name, address, and telephone number. (Consider tattooing and microchip implants that are permanent identification.)

✔ Several stainless steel food and water bowls.

✔ A rack that one or two bowls fit in to prevent Spirit from tipping them over.

✔ A few sturdy rope or nylon toys for her to chew on and play with.

✔ A pad for her to sleep on.

An Akita puppy is happy playing in the snow but needs indoor housing most of the time.

✔ A large plastic dog crate. (Buy the one that will fit her as an adult.)

✔ A stainless steel, wide-tooth comb.

✔ A metal pin brush.

✔ A scissors-type nail trimmer.

Dog Toys

✔ During the past decade, dried, cured pig ears have become popular among some dog owners. They are actually rawhide wafers and like other rawhide toys, may or may not be harmless. Twisted rawhide chew sticks and the similar but larger, rawhide "bones" of various sizes have been popular for many years. Dog owners bought untold numbers of those yummy, flavored, rawhide chewys and many contented canines spent hours chewing them without incident. However, in the past few years, rawhide chewys have received a lot of bad publicity. Veterinary reports indicate that

An Akita needs socialization from the day it is brought home.

soda bottles, without the lids. They entertain the bored individuals for hours and when the bottles are sufficiently wrecked they are picked up and trashed.

✔ Ask your veterinarian about toys for Spirit and follow the professional advice given.

Regardless of your plans for Spirit when she grows up, many other considerations should not be delayed. Spirit is a lovable little teddy bear, a happy, fun-loving little imp. She loves to play, run, and romp with children or adults. She grows like a weed, gradually changing from a roly-poly ball of fur to a gangly awkward teenager within a few weeks and before you know it she is a year old. Watching Spirit mature, physically and mentally, is truly an exciting experience, but your personal interaction during that period is essential.

dogs are often able to swallow those chewsticks, bones, or other rawhide toys, or portions of them, and they may cause gastrointestinal foreign-body problems that require surgical procedures.

✔ Soft, rubber squeaker toys have been around for many years as well and they have always been dangerous because any energetic puppy can destroy them, remove the squeaker valve, and swallow it. They are rarely recommended by health care professionals.

✔ Nylon bones are more durable and can't be swallowed by puppies. They have a texture and taste that dogs enjoy chewing and are easily identified as a dog toy by the least discriminating puppies.

✔ Many longtime Akita owners, including breeders, give their dogs empty 2-liter plastic

Bonding with Your Akita Puppy

Human bonding and family adjustment occur rapidly in young Akita puppies. The period between three weeks and three months of age is the most important human bonding time for Akitas. During that brief period Spirit will form lifelong relationships with her family often becoming strongly attached to the person who gives her the most attention. Akitas acquired before three months will accept correction quickly and easily and the lessons offered will be promptly imprinted on the personalities of those youngsters. That is the time to establish your love for and devotion to your new companion and she will reciprocate.

Even furry puppies should be trained to get along with other dogs.

The quality time that you spend with Spirit, combing and brushing and teaching her what her collar and leash are for is very important to her. She will quickly respond to your care and attention and learn the rules of the household in the bargain. At the same time, you will learn more and more about her character, her likes and dislikes, and the activities that please her the most. This bonding time sets the pace and establishes ground rules for later, more intensive training.

Spirit adds a special dimension to the family environment but raising an Akita puppy is not a spectator sport. The interaction and the lessons learned by your puppy and you are awesome and the key words in that sentence are *you* and *interaction*. You must participate and become a part of the equation. Your children will grow up and be gone after a few years. Your spouse may develop other interests or new projects. You are the one who wanted Spirit and you are responsible for her.

Chewing

Chewing is an unappreciated habit but it is part of being a puppy. Spirit picks up your sock because it has your odor on it. She mouths it to fully identify its nature because it is yours. It smells like you and tastes like you. Socks are more or less expendable but when her sharp little teeth destroy a new shoe or an alligator belt—that is another story.

Have patience and don't lose your sense of humor. Try to remember that mouthing an object is nothing more than a puppy tasting its environment. Chewing clothing is not an activity that should receive undue attention or scolding. Instead, to discourage chewing, speak in a normal volume and tell Spirit *NO!* Have an inviting toy, such as a nylon chew bone handy. Toss it for Spirit to chase or hand it to her and shake it, or hide it, then bring it before her again. When her attention is diverted to the toy, retrieve the article of clothing and put it in

These mischievous Akita puppies are ready for a romp but need human supervision.

a drawer or into the trash can—and remember the incident.

Between four and six months of age, Spirit gradually outgrows her beaverlike need to chew but adolescence brings another surprise. She may forget everything that you taught her previously. That stage quickly passes and soon she will adapt to the family's routine and the restrictions placed upon her. Within a few weeks, she will begin to recognize her toys and differentiate them from other attractive articles.

Socialization

After her vaccination program is finished, socialization begins. Every day, or several times a day, if possible, take Spirit for walks where you know people and their pets gather. Put her in contact with people and animals as often as possible and encourage each friend you meet to speak to her, pet her, and make a fuss over her. Take her for walks in the park where she can see different birds, squirrels, chipmunks, and leashed dogs. Perhaps there is a lake that is populated by ducks, geese, and swans. Those walks interest and amuse her and are part of her animal and human socialization.

Small parking lots where bicycles and grocery carts are found are great adventures for Spirit. If possible, walk by a medical facility where people are in wheelchairs, with walkers, and on crutches. Introduce her to those folks who show interest and allow her to approach and be petted by them.

Professionally monitored puppy kindergarten classes are often sponsored by local dog clubs and are another excellent means of socialization.

If you notice Spirit becoming shy around strangers instead of accepting them, or if she growls at other puppies or adult dogs, contact her breeder for the name of a good professional training consultant. Keep in mind that Akitas characteristically talk; that is, they grunt and make low throat sounds as a means of communication. Spirit isn't always growling but sometimes her conversational method needs explanation.

Living with your Akita puppy is not always easy and sometimes may seem to be a lot of trouble. Puppies piddle and sometimes make horrible messes on the floor. Spirit may chase the cat, track mud on the carpet, chew your shoelaces, and be a general nuisance. You can trip over her or step on her accidentally, and you may find her snoozing on the sofa where she doesn't belong. She will try your patience daily, but make up for all the annoyance she has brought to you with one wag of her tail. She apologetically swipes her wet tongue across your chin when you bend over to fill her water bowl—and all is forgiven. If the thought of minor annoyances and cleaning up after Spirit really bothers you, better buy a goldfish.

Boarding

If you need to board Spirit, check first with her breeder. Sometimes breeders will board dogs that came from their kennel and they appreciate the Akita personality more than anyone else. Think twice before you board her in a commercial kennel because of the stress that is associated with being confined to a cage and small run. Akitas are bored with inactivity and some are antagonized by the confusion and sound of their kennelmates' barking. Odors of females in season often cause excessive barking and growling and are unnerving.

Some boarding kennels are spotless and well managed. Some rotate boarders into large exercise runs, some have pads to lie on, most are built with security and safety in mind. However, not all fit that description and some are dirty hotbeds of kennel cough and flea infestations. Usually you get what you pay for. If you must use a boarding kennel, try to find one with indoor kennels that are divided by solid masonry walls. The kennels should open into runs with solid walls that extend upward for a minimum of 4 feet (1.2 m) from the concrete floor to the chain link fence that divides the covered outside runs.

Luxurious dog hotels are cropping up in many cities. Those facilities are superior to the finest kennels and many offer special diets, stress supplements, grooming, and personal dog-walking services. Those types of facilities are costly but they appeal to the people who want the finest for their pets. If you have a tightly fenced backyard and a good friend who loves your Akita, someone who visits your family often, you might be in luck. That individual might move into your home and dog-sit for you. If you choose that solution, invite the friend to come to your home several times before you leave to feed and play with your Akita in your presence. Spirit is worth the trouble!

TRAINING YOUR AKITA

Never lose your patience with Koby.
Keep lessons short and simple.
Approach each training session
positively and unhurriedly.
Be consistent and never raise
your voice. What is not learned
today will be picked up tomorrow.

Importance of Training

All companion dogs benefit from training but it is even more important in dominant breeds such as the Akita—you owe it to yourself and your neighbors to socialize and train Koby. Use common sense and don't expect him to be totally trained after a week or month. Training is an ongoing effort that will soon show results but will never end.

Set aside ten-minute portions of your morning and afternoon to devote entirely to training and be regular in the endeavor. If you know nothing about dog training, read a book, talk to trainers, ask Koby's breeder for pointers, then proceed. It is important to undertake his training yourself. Don't turn over that duty to a child or a professional trainer. Koby is *your* dog and you can learn to train him.

Akitas are dominant dogs and must
be appropriately trained.

Pick a place and time for training when and where you and Koby will be without distractions, and are alone in the training area. If other family members want to participate, ask them to watch you closely and follow your lead. Everyone should use exactly the same commands, delivered in the same manner, and followed by the same release and reward.

Koby probably doesn't really want to be trained but you can make his schooling pleasant and rewarding for you and your student. When still a puppy his focus time is extremely limited, so repeat a lesson once or twice, then go on to another. Each training session should be kept to no more than ten minutes. You know that he has a short attention span, so when Koby becomes bored with an exercise being taught, switch to one that he has mastered and after he executes it well, end the session.

Important: Never leave a session on a negative note.

Crate Training

One of your first purchases should be a large, plastic, indestructible dog crate with adequate ventilation. Teaching him to use it is one of the first training steps to take.

✔ Put a toy or nylon bone and one of your old, unwashed socks into the crate with his sleeping pad. The sock will have your odor on it and Koby will be more comfortable with the familiar odor surrounding him.

✔ Leave the crate's gate open for the first day to allow him to enter and leave at will.

✔ On day two, place him inside with his chew-toy and sock beside him and give him a small treat as well, then close the gate and quickly walk away. Don't kiss him, wave good-bye, or look back to see if he is okay.

✔ After you have been gone from the room for five or ten minutes, return, open the gate, turn, and walk away.

✔ Don't speak to him or make a fuss over him when he emerges or he will receive a signal that escape is his reward for being confined.

Note: Always give him a treat when he enters the crate but not when he leaves!

✔ Repeat that routine for short periods at odd times during the next few days, and between crating lessons, leave the gate open so he can enter and leave at will. The crate will soon be his den and haven and when he is inside asleep or chewing on a toy he should not be disturbed.

✔ Don't allow children or other pets to tease him anytime, in or out of his crate, and don't abuse the crating time.

✔ He can be crated when you must be away for an hour or two, when you have boisterous children running about the house, when a strange dog is visiting, or when you are cooking or eating and you are training him not to beg.

✔ He can ride in his crate if your car is roomy enough to accommodate it.

Important! You must never crate your dog just to get him out of the way or to punish him. Generally he should never be crated for more than two or three hours at a time except when house-training during the night.

House-training

Akitas are very clean and they try to expel their wastes as far from their beds as possible. However, eliminations are natural events and when the urge to urinate or defecate arrives, untrained puppies respond. Prevention, substitution, and reward are the keys to successful house-training.

✔ Prevention: When Koby arrives at your home, carry him to a particular spot in the yard that you have designated as his toilet area, set him down, and wait until he defecates or

Make sure your crate is big enough for your Akita to stand up and move around in.

A well-trained Akita is a joy to meet.

urinates. Repeat this action each time he becomes restless at night. During the day, put him in his crate (or pen) when you cannot watch him, but never fail to take him out to his toilet area numerous times.

✔ Reward or positive reinforcement: After he has defecated or urinated, verbally praise him while he is still in the toilet area, scratch his head, and pet him, then invite him to follow you back into your house.

✔ Substitution: Each time you see him beginning to circle and sniff, pick him up immediately and carry him to the designated spot in the yard. The odor of feces and urine become impregnated into the grass or soil and soon he will return to that place without fail.

X-pen confinement assists in house-training.

Mistakes and Punishment

If Koby is playing and suddenly realizes that he must urinate or defecate, he may squat without warning. Don't make a major issue of those mistakes and *never* scold him. Instead, pick him up and hurry to his toilet area and when you return, clean up the mess without comment. Use a disinfectant soap that contains no ammonia because when ammonia dries it may smell like urine, therefore its use is counterproductive. *Never* rub his nose in the mess, swat him, or otherwise punish him because those actions will only confuse him and convince him that you are a very strange person—he will never make a connection between your outlandish action and his need to urinate. If you don't want to crate him during the day and you can't monitor his activities, invest in an

X-pen in which to confine him. Place the pen where he will not be isolated from you and the family, cover one end of it with newspaper and in the other end, put his sleeping pad and a toy.

Take him out to his toilet area after every meal, first thing in the morning, last thing before lights out, and anytime he is restless at night. Place his crate beside your bed and leave him in it until he fusses, then carry him outside to his toilet area, wait until he has urinated or defecated, pick him up and take him back to his crate.

Name

Koby was chosen as his name because it is short, is easy to pronounce, and isn't easily confused with any command. Teaching his name is quite simple. Use this technique when he is first fed in your home, and every time thereafter.
• Say *Koby* in a distinct voice.
• Show him his food bowl.
• Set the bowl on the floor.
• Say his name before each command you give him and with the reward when the command is obeyed. *Koby, come. Good dog, Koby.*

Correct training collar placement.

= TIP =

Head Halters

Never leave a head halter on Koby when you aren't with him! They are especially recommended to control dominance and territorial aggression in the book *Dog Training with a Head Halter* by Miriam Fields-Babineau.

Collars and Leashes

Leash training is critical to having a well-mannered Akita. Putting a collar and leash on Koby is the first step in leadership or dominance training. With collar and leash in place, you are in charge and have assumed the pack-leader role. Begin leash training within the first few days of his presence in your home.

Put on his nylon collar and buckle it so that two of your fingers can easily slip between the collar and his neck. Let him scratch and wear it for an hour or two, then fasten a 3-foot (91 cm) piece of light rope or a shoestring to the collar and let him drag it about for a few minutes. The next step is to pick up the loose end of the string and urge him with tidbits to walk beside you. By the time the second training session begins, he will gladly wear his collar and leash because you are walking beside him, and he receives praise and treats when he moves along. As in all training, do not scold or punish Koby for resisting either the leash or collar. Instead, simply continue without comment. At this stage, do not tie him up and leave his presence.

After he has received his immunizations for puppyhood diseases, you can exercise him out of his yard, in the park, on dog walks, or neighborhood sidewalks. Serious obedience training at that time of life is a waste of time but if you have obedience trials in mind for the future, you should put him on your left side when you walk. His identification tag can be attached to his web collar in case he is separated from you accidentally. Rivet the tag to the collar so that it doesn't swing or jingle, which will also prevent it from catching on a branch and being snapped off and lost.

Choke Chain Collars

Those misnamed restraints should be called *training collars*, and should be used when he is older and is being trained more seriously. The chain collar should be removed when he is not being trained. Correct chain collar placement is important. Measure the collar so that it is 2 inches (5.1 cm) longer than Koby's neck circumference. Drop the chain through one of the rings so that a noose is formed with a free ring on one end and the chain sliding through the other ring. Attach the leash to the free ring and put on his collar so that the leash runs up his left side and across the top of his neck and through the other ring. Incorrect placement won't release quickly and may injure your companion. A chain collar that is too long will not close quickly enough to be effective.

Head Halters

The author has not had experience with Akitas using head halters, although he has used them on other, similar-sized, somewhat aggressive and energetic dogs. Judging from that

House-training and routine commands should begin when the dog is a puppy.

experience and the information available, you should try a head halter on Koby. Two head halter types are available: The *Halti* and the *Gentle Leader*. They are essentially equal, but you should talk to your breeder or a trainer to see which is most effective on Akitas. Either head halter should compare very favorably with a training collar because they do not choke, are humane, afford the handler more perfect control, and are safe for a companion pet.

Pronged collars: Pronged collars are inhumane. Something is wrong with your technique and you probably have no business training Koby if you need one of those brutal contraptions to gain control of your companion.

This 10-week-old Akita is just beginning his house-training.

Command Clarity

Each command is separated into distinct parts that are spoken clearly and crisply. Koby has better hearing than you have, so don't shout your commands or repeat them over and over again. Akitas are very trainable and if Koby doesn't respond to his lesson you should reevaluate your technique.

✔ Begin in a quiet environment without distractions.

✔ Get his attention focused on you.

✔ Always begin the command with his name.

✔ Use normal volume and a crisp, authoritative tone.

✔ Make sure he understands what action you are calling for.

✔ Do not confuse him with sentences or multiple word instructions. Never say, "*Koby, come here to me*," or "*please sit down over here*." He

may pick out the words he knows (*come* and *sit*) and react to those words, but he will be confused by extraneous words.

✔ After he responds, release him from the task.

✔ Reward him with praise and a treat.

Basic Commands

Recall (Come): Choose a time when Koby is in the yard or in another room. Prepare his food, then say, "*Koby, come.*" As soon as that command is uttered, use a spoon to tap on the side of his bowl and when you see him running toward you, repeat the "*Koby, come*" command again. When he arrives, set the bowl before him, and praise him. No treats are necessary and you can depend on his response to that command.

Sit: Place Koby before you in a standing position with the wall immediately behind him. Utter the command, "*Koby, sit.*" After that command is given, show him the treat in your right hand, just above his muzzle, and gradually move the treat backward over his head. He will begin to back up, feel the immovable wall, and plunk his bottom on the ground. After he has sat, wait a few seconds, then release him from the command by telling him "*Okay,*" give him his treat, praise, and pet him. Repeat this exercise two or three times and go on to the next lesson or quit for the day.

Note: Koby will probably retain that training better if you do not touch him because he will believe that it was his idea to sit.

Down: This command is also given when Koby is standing before you. Say, "*Koby, sit*"- (hesitate), "*down.*" Then immediately let him smell the treat in your right hand, move it to the ground between his forefeet, and slide it backward. As he tries to reach the treat, he will drop to his elbows and *voila!* he is lying on the ground. Wait a few seconds while his sternum is touching the ground, then release him with "*Okay,*" give him the treat, petting, and praise. Repeat the exercise two or three times, review yesterday's lesson once or twice, pick up his ball, and play for a few minutes.

Stay: After Koby has properly responded to the *sit* or *down* command, instead of releasing him, tell him "*Stay,*" and hold your open right hand, before his face, fingers pointing upward. After he has held his position for a minute, release him with "*Okay,*" and reward him accordingly.

Formal Training

Have you ever seen a proud dog owner grasp a companion's leash, take up the slack, and say "*Heel*"? Your immediate thought is: that is an obedience dog!

Obedience training takes a lot of time and commitment on your part, and a very trainable dog. In order to become proficient in obedience work or any other formal endeavor, enroll Koby (and yourself) in a class.

Obedience work includes many facets of intensive training, from performing simple maneuvering tasks to scent and object identification. You must practice the individual exercises at home, but most of the training occurs when you are with the class. Your instructor teaches you how to train Koby and watches you, corrects your mistakes, makes suggestions, and helps you achieve your goals. Obedience training, show training, agility training, flyball, Frisbee, Freestyle, and other formal and informal training is beyond the scope of this manual

A little fellow picking up some instructions from his sire.

and is left to the experts. If you are interested in formal training, your all-breed or specialty club will aid you. Or you can find references to any of those activities on the Internet.

Positive Reinforcement

Use positive reinforcement to reward each task you ask your companion to perform. A gentle pat on the head or a scratch behind the ears or under the chin will do wonders for Koby's morale. Maintain your cool, always think positively, and finish each training session on an accomplishment. Be liberal with praise and gentle petting and *never* strike Koby when he does something wrong; shouting or waving arms will never work. Akitas can become obstinate or stubborn and when that happens, don't reprimand Koby; instead, walk away and wait a day or two before you resume training and when you resume, do so with a positive attitude.

AKITA ACTIVITIES

Akitas are strong, trainable, outdoorsy, working dogs that thrive on activity. However, the curious Akita plays many roles and often is content to act purely as a companion whose sole function is to please her owners.

Consideration should be given to the planned use of your dog when you choose your Akita. To be merely a pet seems like an inappropriate function for an intelligent, energetic, strong working dog, rather like a rocket scientist working in a diner. Is a companion pet what you really want in your life, or do you expect more from your Akita? You and Spirit can enjoy many activities outside your home if she enjoys training, is an enthusiastic student that focuses on you, and dotes on the time you spend together.

Obedience Trials

Official rules for obedience trials are available on the AKC Web site. That information can be printed and studied and will help you

Akitas are towers of strength and require a good deal of your time.

decide whether or not you and Spirit are ready for the extensive discipline that is required.

It is possible that Spirit is not a satisfactory candidate for formal obedience training. Remember that obedience dogs must perform the *long down* in an obedience ring filled with other dogs, all off-lead. However, especially if she is the progeny of Akitas that have successfully competed in obedience trials, and you are a gentle and clever trainer, give it a try. She may succeed if she has a kind and benevolent temperament and is not overly dominant.

Obedience training is a step-wise progression and you don't jump into off-lead exercises in the beginning. Join a class that is sponsored by your all-breed club or Akita specialty club. In that class, you will be taught to train Spirit and you will be helped to prepare her for each stage of completion of the many obedience disciplines.

Spirit must be six months old before starting in a class and you must have patience and

This solid Akita would be a handful if not well socialized.

belong in such an arena, but an exceptionally trainable Akita with a low dog-aggression personality might compete. In the meantime, attend an agility trial as a spectator. Consult with other Akita owners that know Spirit's personality. Talk with handlers you have met at shows or with trainers who work with agility dogs and follow their advice.

Canine Good Citizen Certificate

A Canine Good Citizen Certificate (CGCC) is an award that is sponsored by the AKC and earned by well-mannered dogs of any breed and their owner-handlers. That coveted diploma certifies that Spirit has successfully reached a level of training and accomplishment that marks her as a well-mannered, trustworthy, and manageable companion dog. It means that you have trained her to act and react to certain events and situations in a calm and obedient manner. It signifies that your determination and commitment to her good behavior have led her to pass the test. You are the trainer, the training required is outlined by the AKC, and the test is administered by specially trained members of local dog clubs. A candidate either passes or fails. No points are awarded; no stages or levels exist. You and Spirit may fail to pass the test a number of times and return to try again. You can start the program at any time and progress at your own (and Spirit's) speed. Most of the exercises are simple to understand and are performed on-lead.

Detailed information on CGCC testing is found on the AKC Web site. Passing the test

perseverance and practice faithfully with her at home. You must have the time and determination and use those qualities in a logical, continuing manner. Keep your training sessions short and develop the ability to detect Spirit's boredom if and when it crops up. Make teaching and learning fun and you may be surprised by your companion's intelligence and trainability, but don't become discouraged if the two of you don't succeed on the first few days.

Agility Trials

Agility is another sport that requires Spirit to totally focus on her companion-handler. Agility trials, like the advanced obedience exercises, are run off-lead and that fact alone may defeat some Akitas because the arena is literally lined with dogs and owners. An assertive Akita doesn't

Show training is a good way to socialize your Akita.

confirms that you are able to control Spirit when you meet a friend on the street or in your home.

1. In one exercise you place Spirit in a sitting position at your side, on lead, and the evaluator pets her on the head and body to test her response.

2. Another test involves her appearance and grooming. The evaluator inspects Spirit's nails, coat, ears, and teeth for cleanliness and she must sit quietly while the evaluator examines her and gently grooms her.

3. In another part of the test you do an about-face while walking her and the evaluator judges her acceptance and response to your leadership. She is kept on-lead and is not expected to heel or walk in a specific relationship to you.

4. Walking through a crowded street or in a mall is another skill that is evaluated.

5. Another relates to her actions and attitude toward bicycles, wheel chairs, and walkers on the street.

6. She is required to come to you when called and react appropriately to a strange dog she encounters with a stranger leading it.

7. The final part of the test is a brief supervised separation from you. You hand the leash to the evaluator, walk away, and return in three minutes.

Do not be tempted to take your young Akita biking.

A fine Akita competing in the famous Westminster show.

Show Akitas must be well socialized with both humans and other dogs.

Weight Pulling and Skijoring

Weight Pulling

You and Spirit may want to take up snow sports if you live in a part of the world that turns white in the winter months. Your local club will advise you of weight-pulling contests that are held in your area. The training requires a canine athlete that is in excellent nutritional and physical condition, and has a strong desire to please her handler. Classes for weight-pulling athletes are held by many all-breed clubs. Pulling dogs must be fully mature and you should remember that Akitas are slow to reach maturity.

Equipment: A special pulling harness is needed and should be custom-fitted to Spirit.

After a few weeks of training she is hitched to a sledge mounted on runners and loaded with standardized weights.

Rules: Rules governing contestants' ages and weights and weights being pulled are posted to be sure that all contests are run competitively. Upon command, a human starter jiggles the sledge to break it loose from the snowy ice and you stand at the finish line and urge Spirit to pull the sledge over a designated distance in a specified time. Pulling contests are great fun for the canine participants and owners alike and the tremendous Akita heart may very well make Spirit a winner.

Skijoring

Skijoring is an equally exciting sport that provides exercise for Spirit and many thrills for you.

A frisky Akita puppy having one last romp in the grass before the training session begins.

No rules are written for this endeavor but some minimal training is required. The dog is fitted with a sledding harness and you don your skis. A rope runs from her harness to your hands, much like the towline used in waterskiing. The rest is up to Spirit and you. Sometimes speed contests are arranged between several dogs and handlers but usually skijoring is a single team sport. Frozen lakes or snow packed trails are the usual courses and spills and thrills are abundant.

Conformation Showing

Another activity for your Akita is the show ring. Showing an Akita can be a rewarding experience. Here is a breed that requires virtually no special grooming, no artificial makeup, and no scissoring or clipping. A bath before the show will suffice; if you invested in a show prospect, you are on the way. Obviously you will need to train and practice with Spirit from the time she is a puppy. By the time she is old enough to join a conformation class she should be comfortable walking on-lead around your home and yard. She should respond to your commands, stand, and move forward at various gaits. She must focus on the handler, ignore the spectators and other dogs in the ring, and tolerate a judge who will open her mouth, check her bite, and lightly pass hands over her entire body. Hours of training time are required before both of you step into a ring before a judge, and most of that time will be spent in class with other handlers and their dogs.

Why should you want to devise ways to occupy Koby's time? Because a bored companion is one step away from being in trouble! Koby needs physical and mental stimulation and challenges to be happy and a joyful companion will make his entire family more contented. Besides, you enjoy taking walks, hiking, and playing games too, so the entertainment is not one-sided. Being together for an hour, an afternoon, or all day means you are tightening the bond between you and your companion.

Playing Catch

Akitas usually aren't great ball players but if you can interest Koby in chasing a ball when young, he may find it an enjoyable game to play all his life. Most young puppies will chase anything that moves and rolling a ball away from them becomes an immediate challenge to stop it and pick it up. However, adult Akitas are apt to turn up their nose at chasing a ball because they can see it has no life of its own, and chasing an inanimate object is beneath their dignity.

✔ Toss a 2-liter empty soda bottle (without the cap and paper label) for Koby to chase and play with. For some reason, the pliable plastic bottle is more interesting to most Akitas than a simple, round ball, and many will toss those bottles in the air for hours every day. When their strong teeth have destroyed the bottle, throw it away and replace it with another.

✔ Soft Frisbees also might be appreciated and Koby may delight in running to catch one that you toss. If he has a retrieving propensity, he may return the Frisbee for you to toss again and again, and if he becomes proficient, you may want to join a Frisbee club and compete formally.

✔ Yard balls are large and reasonably indestructible. They are made to entertain dogs that must stay alone in their backyards for extended periods of time. A yard ball is soccer-sized and too large for Koby to pick up, but if he is bored, he may bat one about with his muzzle for hours every day.

✔ Several manufacturers produce hollow, indestructible cubes that you can stuff with dry kibble. Those feeding cubes usually take hours to empty, during which time Koby will have something interesting to do. Naturally the cubes are of value only if he is fed dry dog food.

Hide and Seek

An Akita's natural possessiveness of toys can be used for entertainment. Have a friend hold Koby's collar

Hide and seek games begin when your Akita is quite young.

firmly, take his favorite toy, show it to him, shake it, then go into another room and hide it for him to find. The game can be expanded to include several rooms, the whole house, and the backyard in accommodating weather. At first, the hiding places should be in relatively plain sight, but after Koby becomes familiar with the game, the toy should be hidden in progressively more and more difficult places to find.

Sniffing Out Objects

Sniffing is a game that can be used to sharpen Koby's scenting ability by using a small piece of cooked, dry meat, or jerky to hide. Have a friend hold him, give him a sniff of the jerky and proceed into the next room and hide it under a rug or behind a door. You will be pleasantly surprised at his excitement and joy when he succeeds in finding, and consuming, the tidbit. Sniffing games also can be expanded to the backyard in pleasant weather.

Socks: Other objects can be used to make the challenge a bit harder. Rob the laundry hamper and retrieve an old sock that you have worn. Give Koby a sniff, then hide it where it is not easily seen, but can be scented out. If he accepts that challenge, hide the old sock in progressively more difficult places. If he is good and finds the sock every time, hide it in a basket of freshly laundered clothes. If Koby finds a used sock in a basket of freshly washed clothes, he is pretty good.

Animal scents: If he becomes adept at finding personal objects that contain family member scents, buy a couple of animal scents in a sporting goods or pet supply store. Put a drop or two of a scent on an object such as a furry piece of tanned rabbit pelt and challenge Koby to find it.

Frisbee playing is one of the Akita's favorite entertainments.

Many dogs can discern and follow objects that have various scents and can differentiate one scent from another. Koby may enjoy that endeavor and if he shows interest and scenting talent, you can expand the idea to actual tracking or search-and-rescue lessons. The Internet is a great place to find search-and-rescue and tracking information.

Roadwork

Walking: Walking is more fun when accompanied by your canine companion. Use Koby's training collar and a strong leash and when walking in a new area, be sure to keep a tight hold on his leash. Find a trail where lots of new smells and sights will occupy him. Take him out early in the cool mornings or late in the evenings. Be certain that you have control of him when you meet other walkers with their dogs. If in doubt, walk him with a head halter, just to be sure. Don't be tempted to exercise Koby alongside your bike or car. One jump at a scurrying bunny and he will end up under a wheel or tangle of spokes and pedals—or worse.

AKITA HEALTH CARE

You decided to acquire an Akita puppy and have already assumed the primary responsibility for her health. Barring a tragedy, that probably means a continuing obligation for more than a dozen years. Don't take that role lightly.

Veterinarians

Veterinary practitioners aren't cloned; they are individually trained over a period of years to help animal owners care for their charges. Many veterinarians specialize in companion pet health and some further specialization in orthopedics, surgery, oncology, ophthalmology, and many other disciplines. They provide a vital service but they aren't all saints. When seeking a veterinarian, be discerning: ask neighbors and friends for referrals, and talk to Spirit's breeder. Try to find a veterinarian in your locality, but drive across town if you need to. If your first choice is not the professional you feel you want to depend upon or if he or she doesn't emanate knowledge, trust, honesty, interest, and cooperation, seek another.

These big Akitas are the picture of excellent health.

Visit as many clinics or animal hospitals as necessary to reach your goal and consider these points:

✔ Is the staff clean, friendly, and helpful?

✔ Is the facility clean and neat?

✔ Does it smell good? Remember that sick animals are in residence and don't expect a rose garden smell.

✔ Is the equipment clean and modern?

✔ Ask the receptionist if other Akita owners are on record, and if not, ask why.

✔ Ask how out-of-hours emergencies are handled.

✔ Ask about overnight patients' stays, how they are handled and monitored.

✔ Acquire a fee schedule for services provided and if one is not available, ask for quotes for a few fees such as office calls, spaying or castration fees, and vaccination charges.

✔ Speak to a veterinarian and ask the practitioner her or his opinion of Akitas. Evaluate the

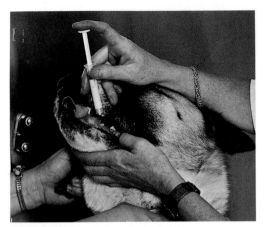

Medication is easiest to administer with a syringe.

respect given to Akita attitudes and personalities, and their individual idiosyncrasies.

A busy practitioner who won't take time to talk to a prospective new client probably won't have time to do a good job and should be scratched off your list. Choose a clinician who is amiable, at ease with your questions, prompt with answers, and one who exudes confidence, knowledge, and a professional attitude. Choose a clinician who has an easy smile, a quiet sense of humor, a firm handshake, and thoughtful, frank answers. Seek a veterinarian who has a great of knowledge but one who is not reluctant to consult with and refer to specialists when needed. Choose a solid, steady individual with practical experience but beware of those who frown when you mention Akitas, or those who have contempt for new ideas and procedures.

First Appointment

If you are comfortable with the facility, staff, and veterinarian, set up an appointment for a new patient evaluation for Spirit. When you pick her up from the breeder, take her directly to your veterinarian for a prepurchase exam. While the doctor is examining her, ask about:

• The parasites found in your area, and the preferred means of preventing infestation of each.

• Heartworm prevention. This is extremely important in most areas of the United States. Be sure you understand the implications associated with the prescribed product.

• Ask about the necessity of Lyme disease prevention.

• Discuss Valley fever and its prevalence in your area.

• Discuss spaying (or neutering) and its importance to your puppy.

• If you anticipate traveling in the future, obtain a boarding kennel referral.

• Ask the professional to teach you to trim Spirit's nails.

• Ask him or her about health insurance for your Akita.

• Ask about the necessity of testing Spirit for hereditary diseases and ascertain whether or not treatment is possible for those diseases if she tests positive for one of them.

The relationship established between you and your Akita's veterinarian will endure for many years and neither you nor the clinician should attempt to speed through that first appointment.

Dental Care

At about six or seven months of age, check Spirit's teeth for retained deciduous teeth. Those will usually be found just outside of or behind the permanent teeth. If that situation occurs, ask your veterinarian to extract them. The significance of retained baby teeth is that they may interfere with the placement of the

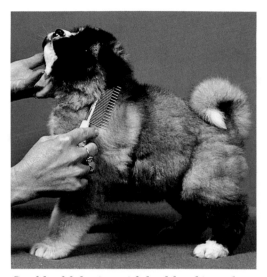

Good health begins with healthy skin and coat in this Akita puppy.

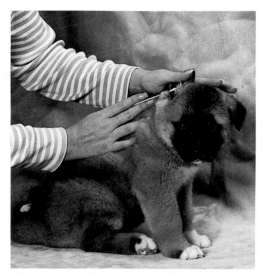

Outer ear flap being cleaned for wax with a swab moistened lightly with alcohol.

permanent teeth. Often they are positioned tightly against the permanent teeth and interfere with the alignment of those teeth. They may become encircled with hair and debris, in which bacteria grow, and gum infection results.

Tartar

Chewing nylon bones and eating a diet of dry kibble will help keep Spirit's teeth and gums healthy. In middle-aged and older dogs tartar and plaque may form on teeth surfaces. If the tartar isn't removed or prevented by brushing and chewing, it must be scraped off, usually under general anesthesia, by your veterinarian. If left in place, the tartar will cause gingivitis (gum infection), the teeth loosen, and sometimes must be extracted. An important side effect of gingivitis is that the bacteria may spread via her bloodstream to her joints, caus-ing inflammation and arthritis, to her kidneys causing nephritis and possibly kidney failure, and to her heart causing myocarditis, which may shorten her life. Tooth brushing should begin early in Spirit's life because it is often much easier to accomplish in a young puppy than in an adult with sore gums from gingivitis.

Ear Care

If Spirit scratches at an ear, shakes her head, and holds it tipped to one side, better have your veterinarian diagnose the problem. She may have a grass awn (foxtail) or some other foreign body in the ear canal, or an ear mite infestation, or a bacterial infection. Never pour any cleaning solution into the ear canal unless a veterinarian checks the ear canal with an oto-scope and advises you which solution to use.

TIP

Vaccines

The best plan is to discuss the vaccine paradox with Spirit's doctor, use common sense and up-to-date information, and vaccinate accordingly.

Eye Care

If Spirit tears excessively, ask your veterinarian to examine her eyelids for entropion, which is a hereditary condition of some Akitas. If affected, the upper or lower eyelids roll inwardly, causing the eye lashes to irritate the cornea (clear portion) of the eye. Entropion can be corrected surgically by your veterinarian. Early diagnosis and treatment is critical!

Regular Veterinary Care

Your veterinarian will keep you apprised of new techniques in preventive medicine, more appropriate immunization plans, and new products available for parasite control. DNA testing is discovering the presence of genetic diseases, new cancer drugs are being developed, and new infectious diseases are being discovered.

You can't keep up with the world of animal health but you can take Spirit to the veterinarian at least once a year for examination and consultation. The time spent with her doctor is invaluable and the results of the visit may extend her happy life. Perhaps the only procedure that may be deemed necessary is a booster vaccination. However, as Spirit ages, the clinician may discover a lump here or a bump there.

Those nodules are explained and recorded for future reference but are not necessarily removed and blood tests may discover an autoimmune condition such as hypothyroidism that can be held at bay by regular administration of a drug.

Vaccinations

Diseases Preventable by Vaccination

Akita vaccination schedules should be formulated for Spirit personally and blanket vaccine recommendations are passé. A logical plan should address the region of the country in which you live and the places you expect to visit with her in the near future. It should consider age, physical condition, other activities in which you are involved that may lead to exposure, and of course her medical history, complete with allergies and sensitivities.

How an Immunizing Agent Works

A vaccine is administered to a healthy Akita to prevent an infectious disease that is caused by a pathogen such as a virus or bacterium. Vaccines may be killed, modified live *pathogens* (germs), or a portion of the pathogen, any of which can act as an *antigen*. Antigens are protein particles, to which the body reacts by producing antibodies. When a vaccine is introduced into a healthy dog's body, it mimics a live pathogen and stimulates the immune system to form antibodies, which destroy that specific pathogen, thus protecting the dog from the disease. When a vaccine is formed by modifying that pathogen, regardless of the virulence (potency) of the pathogen in its natural state, the effectiveness of the vaccine may be reduced.

If Spirit contracts a viral disease and recovers from it, she will probably be immune to that disease for life. Or if she is exposed to a disease after having been vaccinated against it, her immunity will be boosted by the exposure. Likewise, if she receives a single vaccination when she is a puppy, and is not exposed to the causative pathogen and is not revaccinated, her immunity will gradually fade.

Passive Immunity

Antibodies that are formed by one individual and transferred to another will establish a short-term or *passive* immunity to the disease. That immunity is strictly temporary and will last only a few days or weeks. When a vaccinated bitch is pregnant, and delivers puppies, some of her antibodies are furnished to her litter through the placenta (uterine attachment), and more are transferred to puppies in her colostrum (first milk). Those antibodies furnish her puppies with temporary immunity to the disease but they do not stimulate antibodies to be produced by the puppy's immature immune system.

Active Immunity

The opposite of passive immunity is *active* immunity, which confers long-term immunity to a disease. When an antigen is introduced into a healthy dog, the immune system immediately begins to produce antibodies, which in turn neutralize the invading antigen and subsequent invasion by that antigen. A newborn puppy's immune system is not able to respond until about two months of age, but maternal antibodies protect it during that period. That is why a series of vaccinations are administered to newly weaned puppies; the first is given at about eight weeks, and the last of the series is

Vaccine Facts

✔ No vaccine is perfect!

✔ New vaccines are being produced regularly and older vaccines are being changed and improved. Don't rely on what Spirit received last year when considering what she needs this year.

✔ Dogs' responses to vaccines vary between individuals.

✔ Some dogs may not produce immunity from single or multiple vaccinations.

✔ Any vaccine may cause an adverse reaction in any individual dog.

✔ Some vaccines are more stable, potent, and effective than others.

✔ Spirit's physical health and condition affect the degree of protection that a vaccine confers.

✔ A vaccine may interfere with Spirit's immune response to another vaccine when those vaccines are given at the same time.

given at about four months when the puppy's immune system is totally effective.

Vaccination Schedules

Former vaccination schedules recommended vaccinating for all possible pathogens at specific intervals. That is an "overkill" plan that was effective for many years and in many cases, may still be effective.

Testing techniques: Some veterinary practitioners use blood tests to determine the existing level of immunity to diseases, then vaccinate only for those diseases that are known to have a low antibody level. If all testing techniques were identical and if their results were equally reliable, that would be a great plan. Or if people and their pets stayed in

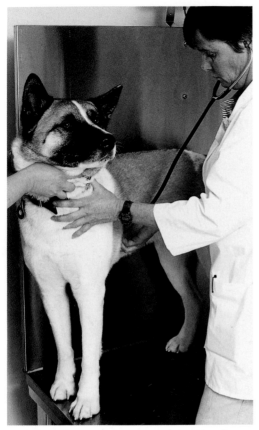

Listening for abnormalities of the Akita's heart.

one location and no new people and pets moved into the location, it would be wonderful. However, lab techniques vary and the results of tests vary. Testing is not totally standardized and we live in a highly mobile society, so strict adherence to the *test-and-vaccinate* plan often does not work as well as it might.

Disease risk: According to the American Veterinary Medical Association and many veterinarians, *disease risk* is the only practical way to address vaccination schedules. If a disease is endemic (present) in your area or if you are traveling to an area where it is found, better vaccinate. Your veterinarian will advise you what product(s) to use and will follow the administration recommendations of the manufacturers.

Booster Vaccinations

Some practitioners claim that boosters are needed only when a blood-titer (antibody concentration level) test indicates a low immunity to specific diseases. Others argue that the cost of testing is greater than the cost of booster vaccines that immunize for many diseases all in one injection.

Core Vaccines

Those vaccines that are deemed by most authorities to be needed by most dogs in most regions of the country are called *core vaccines*. They include
- Canine distemper virus (CD)
- Infectious canine hepatitis (CAV-2)
- Canine parvovirus (CPV)
- Canine rabies

Non-core Vaccines

Dogs living in high-risk areas for certain diseases should consider the administration of the following:
- Canine parainfluenza
- *Bordetella bronchiseptica* (Kennel cough)
- *Leptospira icterohemorrhagia* (Lepto)
- *Borrellia burgdorferi* (Lyme disease)
- Giardia
- Canine Coronavirus (usually not recommended but is available)

Infectious Diseases

That having been said, some infectious diseases are listed below:

Canine Distemper (CD)

Canine distemper is still a deadly threat to unvaccinated dogs partly because of its reservoir among wild canines and partly because its mortality rate is quite high. It attacks young puppies, is without cure, and is easily transmitted. It is primarily a neurological, viral disease that also reduces resistance to bacterial invaders. The signs of distemper often include fever, coughing, greenish yellow nasal and ocular discharge, inappetence (lack of appetite and sluggishness), weight loss, staggering, diarrhea, and later, convulsions and death.

Young, unvaccinated puppies are most susceptible and they often run a high fever, become comatose, and die without any other signs. Some puppies seem to recover but most die within a few weeks. Those that do miraculously recover usually develop tooth enamel defects, facial or extremity twitching, and a thickening and hardening of the foot pads.

Infectious Canine Hepatitis

Canine hepatitis' cause is the canine adenovirus, hence the term CAV-2. It is a potentially deadly infection that attacks the liver and also destroys a puppy's resistance to other diseases. Signs of the disease are similar to those of CD, including sudden death of unvaccinated puppies.

Leptospirosis

This disease has its reservoir among water rodents and is often spread by contaminated river water that the dog drinks. It is caused by an organism called a spirochete that is somewhat like a bacterium, and the kidneys of affected dogs are often totally destroyed by infection. It has been known to affect humans as well as other animal species. Lepto can be treated but the recovered patient often has significant kidney damage.

Parvovirus

Parvo is a contagious disease that is often fatal. It is easily spread by feces and other bodily discharges, is highly resistant to disinfectants, and may survive for many months in dog feces. It causes high fever, dehydration, bloody diarrhea, vomiting, and heart complications. Intensive therapy may save a patient's life but aftereffects may be significant.

Coronavirus

Corona is similar to parvo in that both can cause bloody diarrhea and vomiting, general

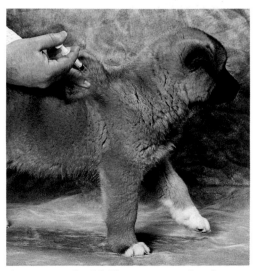

A seven-week-old Akita receiving his first vaccination.

malaise, and death in many affected puppies or adults.

Lyme Disease

Blood-sucking parasites such as ticks are the vectors (carriers) for this zoonotic disease (affecting humans as well as animals). It causes nonspecific, generalized pain, joint pain and swelling, fever, lymph node swelling, and vague generalized illness.

Kennel Cough

This disease got its name from boarding kennels but it isn't confined to kennel residents. It is spread by airborne particles, often sneezes and coughing of an infected dog. Kennel cough frequently is caused by a combination of bacterial and viral pathogens such as parainfluenza virus and Bordetella bacteria. It causes a chronic, honking cough that may continue for many weeks. No specific therapy will cure kennel cough but ignoring this condition may lead to pneumonia.

A seven-week-old Akita puppy having his nails trimmed for the first time.

Canine Influenza

Canine flu apparently is a new disease of dogs that was studied in Florida early in 2004 in greyhounds at a racetrack and since has been identified in a number of other states. In its earliest stages, flu mimics the common, milder condition known as Kennel Cough but flu may be fatal if not treated aggressively. In its usual course, respiratory signs may be seen for about three weeks before recovery. Severe cases develop pneumonia, a high fever (106°F, 41°C) and despite aggressive therapy, the patient may suffer respiratory distress and death. Spread is rapid by aerosol from sneezing and coughing and by objects that have been contaminated by a coughing, sneezing host. Flu is often seen in dogs that have recently been exposed to an area of high concentration of dogs such as boarding kennels but it can result from a coughing dog you meet while walking Spirit. No vaccine is available at this time and no spread to humans has been documented. Your veterinarian can send blood samples from suspected dogs to a laboratory for positive identification.

Rabies

Rabies is a fatal, systemic, neurological, zoonotic disease of all warm-blooded animals. The rabies virus invades the salivary glands of an infected animal and paralyzes the throat. It is transmitted from one animal to another through the host's infected saliva and typically when bitten by a rabid animal. Reservoirs are found in wild animals such as coyotes, skunks, raccoons, bats, rats, ferrets, and mink. It is also found in domestic animals such as cattle, dogs, and cats. If a human is bitten by a rabid animal, immediate medical treatment is necessary to stop the infection.

Other Serious Diseases and Health Problems

Heatstroke

Heatstroke is a serious threat to a heavily coated Akita. Prevention is always better than treatment and that fact is critically important to understand. Heatstroke can occur even in mild weather if a dog is closed in a car in the sun, because a car sitting in the sun will act like an oven and the temperature can reach enormous heights. A dog's temperature may go from a normal of 101 to 105°F (38.3–40.5°C) and sometimes up to 110°F (43.3°C). Respiration becomes rapid and labored, panting begins, and the dog exudes thick, stringy saliva. Mucous membrane color changes from pink to bright red, soon turns pale and bluish before the dog becomes comatose and, without immediate treatment, will die.

Treatment: First aid involves cooling the affected dog with water from a garden hose or placing her in a tub of cool water. Do not use ice to cool her because the ice will cause blood vessels to constrict, delaying the water's effect. If the patient is awake, encourage drinking. Intravenous fluids and other shock therapy is more effective but heatstroke rarely allows the owner time to seek professional help.

Hot Spots

Hot spots are localized, infected skin lesions that occur because of some irritation such as a flea bite. Spirit licks the spot, which dampens

---

TIP

Heatstroke Prevention
- Do not take your Akita in the car unless she can leave it when you do.
- Be sure she has plenty of water in her backyard, kennel, run, house, or wherever she is kept.
- Furnish her some type of shade if she is left outside.

---

her coat and she continues licking until serum oozes. Bacteria begin to multiply in the moist, warm, oozing lesion, resulting in a hot spot. Therapy is usually straightforward and sometimes includes an anti-inflammatory injection, shaving the lesion, and application of antibiotic creams and drying agents.

Arthritis

Arthritis is joint inflammation that might be initiated by injury, hereditary diseases, or old age deterioration. It can occur in any joint of the body but often is first recognized in hips, elbows, and spine. Obesity often exacerbates the condition. After diagnosis, it may be treated by a number of oral or injectable anti-inflammatory medications.

Allergies

Allergies are common to most canines and may be caused by ingested food or physical contact with allergenic substances. Food allergies may cause gastric upsets or they may be manifested by itching, skin redness, and other topical problems. Allergic reactions can be pre-

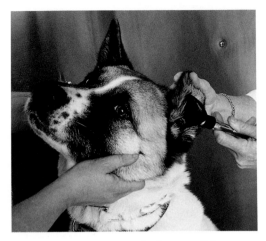

Searching for a grass awn in an Akita's ear.

vented in many cases, and when possible, prevention is preferable to treatment.

Grass Awns

Grass awns or foxtails are pesky and can cause grief if Spirit goes for a walk where they are found. Small seedpods lodge in her ear canals, under her eyelids, between her toes, in her nose or throat, and just about any other place on her body. They often penetrate the skin and become imbedded into her tissues and must be removed under sedation. Don't take awns lightly because they can migrate deeply and cause serious complications if not removed promptly.

Valley Fever

Valley Fever, the scientific name of which is *Coccidioides immitus* causes a zoonotic fungal infection. The microscopic spores of the organism are found most commonly in the desert regions of the southwestern United States. Fungal spores are almost indestructible and they remain dormant in the soil for eons but become viable when they invade a satisfactory host. They may be carried by wind, ingested, or

inhaled. The organism reproduces in the host's tissues causing lethargy, joint pain, tenderness, lameness, respiratory distress, and a litany of other signs. The disease is sometimes difficult to diagnose, and very difficult to treat and often, relief requires medication for many months.

Gastric Dilatation and Volvulus

GDV or Bloat can be a devastating condition if it isn't recognized promptly and treated aggressively. Theories abound relative to the cause of this serious condition. GDV may be precipitated by a number of factors:

✔ Large dogs with a voracious appetite that engorge rapidly.

✔ Feeding one large meal each day.

✔ Feeding unmoistened, dry kibble.

✔ Allowing free access to water immediately following meals.

✔ Exercise and excitement within an hour of a big meal.

✔ Allowing the dog to eat from the floor level. (Some claim that food dishes should be elevated to chest height but the benefit of that is presently being debated.)

✔ The most interesting footnote to this list is Purdue University's veterinary study, which suggests that dogs that have happy, well-adjusted temperaments may be less apt to develop GDV.

GDV begins about two to six hours after eating a meal. The condition is always an emergency and Akita owners should be aware of the signs and the reasons for immediate veterinary intervention. GDV often is fatal if it is not recognized and treated quickly. Signs include

• Bloating, especially on the left side, behind the rib cage.

- Difficulty breathing and stringy saliva drooling from the mouth.
- Frequent unproductive vomiting attempts.
- Oral mucous membrane color darkens.
- Disorientation and staggering.

Coma and death may follow within an hour of onset of the symptoms.

Caution! If GDV is suspected, contact an emergency veterinary service immediately!

Hereditary Diseases

A host of congenital, hereditary diseases are known to exist in the Akita and they include:

Canine hip dysplasia (CHD): This an important threat to all Akitas. It is a debilitating condition that may not cause symptoms until adulthood and is hereditary in a complex way. For many years, breeders and veterinarians have tried to establish puppy examination procedures to diagnose the condition before the puppies are sold. The most reliable diagnostic techniques use radiographic examination (X-ray) of the hips of adults that are more than two years old. The Orthopedic Foundation for Animals (OFA), and The University of Pennsylvania Hip Improvement Program (PennHIP) are the two certifying organizations and the one you choose will study Spirit's X-rays, which are taken by your local veterinarian while she is under anesthetic. The certifying organization sends its report to you and your veterinarian, and will classify Spirit's hips as normal or not normal. When bitches with normal hips are bred to males with normal hips, the puppies born to those dogs are more likely to have normal hips. However, several generations of normal to normal breeding are required to eliminate this horrible hereditary condition

from a bloodline. Even when many generations of certified normal dogs are used in the gene pool, an occasional dysplastic dog will be produced. Selective breeding is the only way to eliminate this hereditary disease that is present in about 10 percent of all Akitas.

The secondary arthritis debility and pain that occurs with CHD is related to the degree of abnormality of the hip joint and the weight and age of the Akita involved. In some cases, the pain can be surgically alleviated by artificial hip implants but the cost of such surgery may be prohibitive.

CHD is an important disease that warrants the attention of all Akita owners and that is the best reason why you should buy your Akita puppy from a breeder who has all parents certified free from hereditary diseases.

Autoimmune diseases: These are also hereditary and include hypothyroidism (reduced thyroid function), which is possibly one of the greatest threats to the Akita, but the good news is that the disease is treatable. *Pemphigus foliaceus* (skin disease) is another hereditary condition, as is hemolytic anemia (loss of hemoglobin from the red blood cells).

VKH: Vogt, Kuyanagi, Harada's disease is a skin and eye disease that can lead to blindness.

Thrombocytopenia (blood clotting failure).

Epilepsy (seizure disease).

Chondrodysplasia (dwarfism): This is seen in Akitas in increasing numbers.

Hereditary Eye Diseases

✔ Entropion, which is an inward-rolling of the eyelids that can be surgically corrected.

✔ Glaucoma (increased pressure within the eye) is a more serious disease and although it may be controlled with surgical procedures and

medical therapy, it can cause your companion's life to be shortened.

✔ Progressive retinal atrophy (PRA) is an irreversible wasting disease of the retina. Members of the American College of Veterinary Ophthalmologists (ACVO) will examine Spirit's eyes and indicate any diseases found. The Canine Eye Registry Foundation (CERF) includes purebred dog owners and breeders and registers those dogs that have been found free from ocular disease and certified by ACVO. DNA testing for Akita PRA carriers will be possible within a short time.

✔ Microphthalmia (congenitally small eyes) is a congenital condition in which Akita puppies are born without vision.

Parasites

Facts about parasites that surround and often confound owners are becoming more complex each year. Consult your veterinarian to decide which of the various control plans is best suited

A well-groomed Akita displaying her beauty for all to see.

to Spirit. Do not visit an Internet site for advice without first talking to Spirit's doctor to establish which parasites are present in your area and what products you should use for safe, commonsense parasite control. Do not try to diagnose, treat, or prevent parasites on your own because one product may interfere with the actions of another. Products have been developed that control several different parasites in a single medication. Several are oral products and others are applied to her skin, but many hoaxes and antiquated methods of parasite control also exist.

Endoparasites are those that live within the Akita's body at the host's expense.

✔ **Roundworm** larvae can be transferred from an infested, pregnant dam to her puppies before they are born. Those larvae migrate through the puppies' tissues, reach the lungs, are coughed up and swallowed, and the adults take up residence within the host's intestinal tract. They lay eggs that pass out in the puppy's feces, and are spread to other dogs by ingestion. Diagnosis is made by microscopic examination of the host's feces (fecal exam).

✔ **Hookworms** are blood-sucking intestinal worms that are smaller than ascarids but also cause significant damage to their hosts. Their eggs pass out of the gut and hatch, and those larvae penetrate the skin of hosts, migrate through the host's tissues until they reach their home in the gut. A heavy infestation may cause anemia or even death.

✔ **Tapeworms** are a two-host parasite. The adult tapeworm attaches its head (scolex) to the lining of the gut; its segmented body grows to immense lengths. The segments break off, pass from the gut, and are picked up by secondary hosts such as fleas or animals such as deer. A dog consumes the tissues of the secondary host, together with a tapeworm cyst, which produces many adult tapeworms that attach to the gut lining.

✔ **Heartworms** cause major damage to their host. The adult heartworm grows to many inches in length, lives within the heart's chambers or large blood vessels, and produces living larvae. The physical presence of a heavy heartworm infestation can cause serious compromise to the host's heart. When a mosquito sucks blood from an infested dog, the larvae of the heartworm *Dirofilaria immitis,* are picked up by the insect and are injected into new hosts.

Ectoparasites are those that live on the exterior of your Akita and they include

✔ **Mites** are microscopic, eight-legged pests that burrow beneath and within the skin of their hosts. They cause hair loss, redness, itching, serum oozing, and are a source of extreme irritation to the host. There are several genera of mites, each of which prefers a different region of the host's body. *Cheyletiella, Demodex, Psoroptes,* and *Sarcoptes,* are diagnosed by taking a skin scraping and viewing it under a microscope.

✔ **Fungus** (*Microsporum canis*) infestations are usually found on the belly skin and may appear as a circular, raised, red lesion, hence their common name, which is *ringworm.*

✔ **Fleas** are the most common ectoparasite; their control is not simple but advancing technology is closing in. They are tiny, white insects that live both on their host's body and in the host's environment. Flea infestations are worse in warm, high-humidity regions but can be found virtually everywhere, except perhaps in

Fleas are one of the secondary hosts for tapeworms.

mountainous, chilly climates. A flea bites the host and laps up the oozing serum, causing significant irritation. Flea saliva is very allergenic, and the host may react violently to a flea bite.

Adult fleas are found primarily on Spirit's back and you may be able to see them hopping about on her fur. The plush nature of an Akita's coat may act as a natural barrier to flea infestation but don't count on it. The mighty flea is not terribly particular where it receives its blood meal, so don't be surprised if one hops on your arm and takes a taste of your blood. Adult female fleas mate and lay eggs, which drop and molt on the ground or floor, eating whatever organic material is available (including tapeworm segments). After several molts, the adult flea emerges and seeks a viable host and the whole cycle begins again.

Removing a Tick

1. To remove a tick, put on a pair of latex or latril gloves.
2. Dampen Spirit's hair with alcohol, and with a pair of blunt tweezers or hemostat forceps, grasp the tick as close as possible to its skin attachment.
3. Pull the tick slowly, using gentle but firm pressure. When its head emerges, drop the tick into a vial of alcohol, which will kill it.
4. Don't handle it with bare fingers, don't crush it, don't toss it on the ground or in a waste basket, and don't burn it.

✔ **Lice** also live on the skin and feed on the blood of their hosts but are more easily controlled. All life stages of the louse live on the host, laying their eggs (nits) on the dog's hair where they may be seen with the aid of a magnifying glass.

✔ **Ticks** can be seen with your naked eye. The female tick attaches to the skin, buries her head, and drinks blood, which causes her body to swell to the size of a grape. Male ticks are tiny and may be found alongside the female, attached to the host's skin. The engorged female drops to the ground or floor, and lays hundreds of eggs, which hatch and molt twice to become adults. Each of the three life forms of the tick must suck blood from a host in order to progress to the next stage. Most ticks require two or three different hosts, usually of different species—one for the adult, one for the larva, and one for the nymph.

The hardest tick to control is *Rhipcephalus sanguineus,* or brown dog tick, because all forms of that parasite feed on a single species, the canine. Ticks act as vectors (carriers) for various diseases such as Lyme disease, which can be transmitted to humans as well.

The skin lesion that remains should be cleaned daily for a few days to prevent infection. Make note of the date the tick was removed and if Spirit becomes lethargic or acts sick at a later date, consult your veterinarian.

Breeding

Why Not Breed Your Akita?

Reputable Akita breeding is a specialized endeavor that requires a great deal of technical knowledge and research. It is far more complex than simply introducing a vigorous mature male to a healthy female in season and waiting 63 days for puppies to appear.

A good rule of thumb is that if you bought your female Akita from a knowledgeable, reputable Akita breeder as a show and breeding prospect, and if she has earned the recognition of judges in dog shows, she may possibly be a worthy brood bitch. If she was bought as a companion pet, the chances are she should not be bred. Obviously, if you own a male Akita, the same minimal precautions apply. Keep in mind that an unworthy female might contribute a dozen puppies to the world each year, but a male could breed 100 females and produce thousands of puppies in the same period.

Reasons for Not Breeding Your Akita

✔ Breeding and raising puppies is expensive and includes show fees, handler fees, trans-

A beautiful, healthy, happy, well-socialized Akita.

portation charges for shipping her to out-of-town shows and eventually, a stud fee.

✔ Costs of veterinary bills for a brood bitch and her litter are very significant. Consider Spirit's various examinations for hereditary conditions, and her puppies' examinations, vaccinations, worm treatment, and food.

✔ The risk of cesarean section delivery of puppies is significant and emergency surgery is costly.

✔ High risks are associated with pyometra (uterine infection) and mammary cancer in an intact female.

Reasons for Spaying Your Female Akita

Spaying refers to the surgical operation (ovariohysterectomy), in which both of the bitch's ovaries and the uterus are removed. It can be done as early as a few weeks after she has received her puppy vaccinations, and is strong and in good health.

✔ Spaying Spirit before her first estrus period has been proven to reduce the risk of developing mammary cancer and pyometra to virtually zero.

✔ Spaying prevents three-week-long estrus periods that usually occur every six months.

✔ Spaying negates boarding charges each time Spirit comes into heat.

✔ Spaying may calm a nervous or aggressive bitch.

✔ Spaying does not cause obesity. Overweight female Akitas are those that are overfed, underexercised, or suffering from dietary or hormone imbalances.

✔ Surgical fees are lowest in young bitches before their first heat.

✔ Spaying when young and in good health is recommended because of the risk involved with general anesthetic in an obese, older female.

Reasons for Castrating (Neutering) Your Male Akita

Castration means surgical removal of both testicles. The procedure is not the same as a vasectomy and it renders the Akita sterile and impotent. The procedure rarely stops territorial marking.

• If the procedure is performed before sexual maturity it reduces the risk of prostate cancer to zero.

• Castration prevents testicular cancer.

• Neutering may calm a nervous or aggressive male and may stop his wandering.

• Neutering does not cause obesity. Overweight male Akitas are overfed, underexercised, or suffering from dietary or hormone imbalances.

Grooming Equipment

- Canine toothbrush and toothpaste
- Stainless steel comb with wide-set teeth
- Spray bottle filled with plain water
- Metal pin brush
- Scissor-type nail trimmer
- Styptic stick, powder, or liquid
- Electric hair dryer with warm setting
- Bathtub with a sprayer hose attached and a hair catcher in the drain
- Rubber tub mat
- Bottle of an emollient dog shampoo
- Stack of dry towels
- Cotton balls
- Hydrogen peroxide
- Tube of petrolatum jelly
- Blunt-tipped scissors

Use sharp nippers and take thin slices when trimming nails.

Teeth

Brush several times a week. Tartar and plaque can be prevented by brushing Spirit's teeth two or three times weekly. Use a special canine finger brush and canine toothpaste, both of which are available in pet supply stores. Apply the paste to the brush and rub her teeth. Do not use human toothpaste because Spirit won't appreciate its minty flavor. Canine toothpaste tastes like meat and Spirit probably won't resist its use.

With this procedure, do not open her mouth. Hold her jaws closed and run your finger inside of her lips on the outside surface of the teeth. Massage each side for a couple of minutes. When starting, just use your finger with no brush. When she is comfortable with that process, add the brush and toothpaste.

Toenails

Spirit's nails should be checked every couple of weeks, but they may wear away with exercise and hardly ever require your attention. When they need to be trimmed, look closely at Spirit's nail conformation. You will find that a toenail is hollow, rather like an inverted V

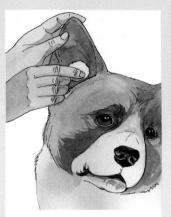

Never insert a swab into the ear canal.

near the point. The nail is solid toward its attachment and that portion contains blood vessels and nerves (the *quick*). Use a sharp, scissor-type nail trimmer and snip off the tip end, then take another thin slice, and proceed toward the quick in that manner. Stop trimming when the cross-section of the cut edge is solid and somewhat soft. If one of Spirit's nails is white or colorless, you can see the quick and stay away from it.

Note: Slight bleeding may occur if you trim one of Spirit's nails too short but it isn't the end of the world. She will wince and possibly yelp and you will see a drop of blood on the cut edge of the nail. Put pressure on the cut edge with your finger and hold it there until you can moisten the end of a styptic stick, press it against the bleeding nail edge, and hold it there for a several minutes. The pain and bleeding will last for only a few seconds and Spirit won't hold a grudge.

Eyes

Check daily; clean when needed. Clean any mucous secretion from Spirit's eyes with a cotton ball moistened with warm water. Before bathing, put a tiny amount of petroleum jelly on the surface of her eyes to protect them from soap irritation.

Ears

Check weekly or when irritated and clean monthly. Ear cleaning is rarely much of a chore in erect-eared breeds like Spirit. If you notice a significant amount of wax or dirt in her outer ear canal it can easily be cleaned with a cotton ball moistened with hydrogen peroxide. Before bathing Spirit, twist two cotton balls into cords about 1 inch (2.5 cm) long and put a cotton cord into each ear to prevent large quantities of soapy water from entering the ear canals.

Bathing

✔ Spray her undercoat with a fine mist of plain water to dampen it and make it easier to brush and comb. That will also prevent the soft fine hair from flying in the air, getting into your eyes, being inhaled, and tickling your nose.
✔ Place Spirit in the bathtub, standing her on the rubber mat to prevent slipping and falling.
✔ Set the water temperature so it is tepid, neither hot nor cold.

Bathing an Akita demands time, patience, and cooperation.

✔ Hold the sprayer hose attachment close against her skin and move it across her body, neck, underbelly, and legs.
✔ After her skin and coat are thoroughly soaked, turn off the water and gradually work up a lather with the shampoo.
✔ Work the lather into her coat over her entire body, and when finished, turn on the tepid water again and begin rinsing in the same manner you used when soaking her.
✔ Go over her body several times, rinsing all the soap from her coat, until clear water is emerging.
✔ Towel Spirit, changing towels until they are no longer absorbing water, and are only damp.
✔ Turn on the electric hair dryer (low setting) and spend the necessary time to thoroughly dry Spirit.
✔ Brush and comb her coat continuously while using the dryer to hasten the drying process. Have patience because an adult Akita that is in full coat may require an hour or more to dry due to the absorbency of her hair. If a tangle is discovered while working with comb, brush, and dryer, the knot can be teased apart, or cut from her coat with a pair of blunt scissors.

FEEDING YOUR AKITA

What, how much, and when to feed Koby are some of the most important questions that a new Akita owner can ask because your puppy's diet is the basis for his appearance, health, and practically every facet of his life. His growth, strength, and physical and mental development are reflections of his diet from birth to death.

Dietary Needs

As Koby's patron you must have an understanding of his nutritional needs and a plan to provide those dietary necessities. Many Akitas are found to suffer from dietary allergies, and if an allergy is diagnosed, that sensitivity must be addressed by his veterinarian. However, a healthy, nonallergic Akita is a relatively easy keeper.

An in-depth, technical consideration of canine nutrition is beyond the scope of this owner's manual. Most pet owners want to know what dog food is best to buy; they don't want to read the details of enzyme interaction with protein, digestion of carbohydrates, or the assimilation advantage of feeding animal fatty acids or animal amino acids instead of those of vegetable origin.

Your Akita's condition and activity reflect its nutritional state.

Ingredients

Labels of all dog foods must list the ingredients in the order of the highest to the lowest amounts contained in the product. Dogs are not true carnivores; they are omnivores like humans and will live happier and healthier lives when given a diet that contains both animal and vegetable ingredients; however, Akitas generally do not prosper on soy-based dog foods. Koby's taste preferences probably are similar to other Akitas, but not necessarily. Akitas usually enjoy the taste of fish and thrive on meat products, but those items should not be added to an already balanced diet that contains the proper amounts of protein, fat, and carbohydrate. When you pick a food for Koby, you have a choice and can select the one that seems best to you according to its label and is best accepted by your companion. His total daily dietary need increases when he is being regularly worked, trained hard, or is under

*This little fellow no doubt belongs
to nutrition-conscious owners.*

body. That chore is accomplished by his salivary enzymes, stomach acid, liver bile, enzymes present in his food and those produced by his abdominal organs such as the pancreas. If he eats dry dog food exclusively, he will consume more water for proper digestion than if he were fed canned food because dry food contains very little moisture. Dehydrated foods contain even less moisture. His water consumption will be at its lowest if he is young and healthy, normally active, living in a moderate climate, and eating canned dog food, which is often more than half water. The obvious problem with feeding canned food is the cost of buying all that water! You can compare canned food to dry food by studying the dry weight of ingredients of the two types of food.

stress associated with rapid growth, illness, or injury. A pregnant female also is under considerable nutritional stress.

The National Research Council (NRC) is a body that publishes an excellent, inexpensive booklet containing technical canine nutritional information that may be purchased by calling 1-800-624-6242. If you want more complete information, please read that booklet.

Water

Water is essential for life. Koby needs a constant source of pure, clean, fresh water. The amount he needs depends on the environmental ambient temperature, his activity level, age, health status, and diet. All food must be broken down, emulsified, and transformed into slurry or liquid form in the stomach and intestinal tract before it can be absorbed and used by his

Commercial Dog Foods

As you can tell, dog foods are not all alike. Types of dog food include dry, canned, and semimoist. Dry dog foods are usually the least expensive type and easiest to feed but you get what you pay for.

Canned foods vary according to their contents and prices but they have one thing in common: they contain up to 70 percent water. In a big dog like Koby, canned foods may cause gastric upsets because of the high water content.

Semimoist (pouched) foods are dehydrated and they are often dangerous because of the amount of water that must be consumed in order to rehydrate them. They also contain some chemicals that may cause allergic reactions.

The hundreds of different brands baffle consumers and veterinarians alike. Prices and ingredients aren't even similar, and comparison is difficult. Don't visit a store without a calculator,

TIP

Food

✔ Never overfeed an Akita puppy. A fat puppy is not a healthy puppy and overfeeding can precipitate physical deformities.

✔ Consider the quality of food, not just the price.

✔ Don't change food without good reason.

✔ Don't feed your puppy a food that is designated as an "NRC maintenance diet," because it is designed for normal adults and not youths.

✔ If a label doesn't have an AAFCO declaration, call the toll-free number on the package and ask about feeding trials.

✔ Call for specific information about a food's source of protein, fat, and carbohydrate if that information does not appear on the label.

✔ Always start with a small bag of food to check it with Koby's palate before you invest in a large economy package.

pencil, and paper to make notes. Premium dry and canned foods are at the top of the price heap, brand name foods that have been around for years are next, and last are the generic or house brands.

Premium Brands

Premium brands often contain the highest-quality ingredients and they are the most reliable year-round dog foods. However, *premium quality* doesn't necessarily mean the *newest* brand of food on the shelf because some of the older and better-known companies produce excellent premium foods. Palatability is important and taste often increases with the price paid; however, lower-priced brand name foods may be as palatable as higher-priced premium foods, and in many cases they are nearly nutritionally identical as well.

Understanding Dog Food Labels

✔ AAFCO stands for the American Association of Feed Control Officials, an organization that consists of canine nutritionists who sponsor feeding trials.

✔ Amino acids are protein components.

✔ Bioavailability is the digestibility of a food element.

✔ Calories refer to the amount of energy contained in a given amount of the food.

✔ *Complete and balanced* means that the food can be fed without adding any supplements.

✔ Crude fat is the amount of animal and plant fat contained.

✔ Crude protein is the amount of animal and plant protein.

✔ Fatty acids are the components of animal or plant fats.

✔ Ingredients are always listed in order of largest to smallest amount contained.

✔ Moisture content is the amount of water contained.

Types of Diets

Puppy foods are specifically formulated for growing puppies and are meant to meet the needs of pups from weaning to adulthood without adding any supplements.

This fine brindle and white male Akita is enjoying some cold weather.

Maintenance rations furnish all the necessary dietary elements for dogs' lives between one year or 18 months of age and upward.

Stress formulas contain ingredients that are meant to boost the resistance and general health of an injured, ill, pregnant, or hardworking Akita during the time of an extra nutritional burden. They contain higher than normal bioavailable nutrients to reduce the total amount of food needed.

Geriatric diets are formulated for old dogs whose organs are beginning to deteriorate, who are not effectively absorbing the nutrients that are present in adult diets, and those who need a little extra nutritional help.

Supplements

Supplements are additive products such as fatty acids, amino acids, vitamins, minerals, and sometimes enzymes. They are rarely necessary if Koby's diet is carefully chosen and fed in appropriate amounts. Don't feed supplements unless advised to do so by Koby's health professional because certain vitamins such as A and D (fat-soluble vitamins) may accumulate in his system and become detrimental to his health. Calcium can also cause a great deal of mischief if fed in larger than normal quantities.

Treats

Most commercial treats have calories and usually are harmless unless fed in excessive amounts. They are helpful when training Koby and sometimes just because you want to offer a little extra love to your companion. Use your head and don't reward Koby too liberally. Commercial treats are packaged with the same label requirements as dog foods.

Table Scraps

Leftovers from your table can be dangerous for Koby for a number of reasons:
• The sugar or salt content of human foods can cause digestive problems.
• Milk left over from your cereal may cause diarrhea.
• Meat or fish scraps, sweets, and gravies are high-calorie products that will throw Koby's diet out of balance and may be a primary cause of obesity.
• Seasonings that do not upset your stomach may react violently in Koby's digestive system.
• Scraps may cause allergies, skin problems, and vitamin and mineral deficiencies.

Obesity in Akitas

Overfeeding your companion will shorten his life. Obesity will contribute to mental and physical problems. Excess weight may cause or exacerbate heart problems, arthritic joints, skin diseases, and systemic diseases such as diabetes.

Akita showing no signs of feeding problems.

Overweight Akita puppies may suffer developmental bone and joint problems. Adult Akitas often are satisfied with less exercise than some breeds and reduced exercise means less food! If you allow your companion to eat table scraps and reward him with tons of treats, he will undoubtedly be obese.

How Much Food?

Unfortunately, the directions on a sack of maintenance dog food can't be trusted. Those instructions are generic and written to fit all dogs' dietary needs—but Koby's caloric intake should be governed by his condition, not a general statement made by someone who doesn't know him. Feed him slightly less than the printed recommendations and weigh him weekly. If he is losing weight, increase his intake, and if he is gaining, cut back a bit. He should be strong, playful, active, mentally alert, curious, and ready for action. If he is frequently lethargic, disinterested, or less energetic than you feel is normal, he may be suffering from nutritional imbalance. If in doubt, ask your veterinarian's opinion.

You can estimate Koby's condition by palpating (feeling) his chest. The skin over his rib cage should be supple and not stretched tightly. When a skin fold over his withers (shoulder blade area) is picked up between your fingers, then released, it should bounce back immediately. His ribs should be quite evident to your touch but covered with a thin layer of fat. If you can barely feel them, he is too fat. If they are quite prominent and not covered with a thin fat layer, increase his food intake.

Koby should step back from his food pan when it is empty. It is not normal for a healthy Akita to leave some food in his dish and if he does so, you are probably feeding too much. It is normal for him to finish his meal and lick the bowl but he shouldn't search for more food. If he does, weigh him and consider increasing his intake with the next feeding. Don't give him more food immediately.

How Often?

✔ Puppies from weaning to about six months of age should be fed three times daily.
✔ Active youths that are in heavy training or under other stress can continue to be fed three meals.
✔ Adults over one year of age should be fed twice daily.
✔ Geriatric pets should be fed two or three times daily depending on their condition and your veterinarian's advice.

OLD AKITAS

If everyone can agree on one subject, it is that we are all getting older each day and nothing can be done about it except to die. With that fact in mind, certain ideas and plans can make getting old a little easier for our valued companion.

Senile Dementia

Spirit often wanders aimlessly, as if she doesn't know exactly where she is. Old dogs, like old humans, suffer from dementia, forgetfulness, and lack of bowel or urinary control. Have patience and don't scold her if she soils the floor occasionally or changes her other habits.

Physical Examinations

Spirit has had numerous physical exams throughout her life and her old age presents new reasons for those veterinary visits. Her coat is not as plush and beautiful as in her youth, but her attitude is still good. She bumped into a chair that you recently bought for the living room but maybe that was simply carelessness. Her exercise and activity has been

This old-timer deserves the best in her declining years.

decreasing for a few years. She labors to arise first thing in the morning and spends more time lying around. She doesn't have hip dysplasia but seems to be stiff in her hind legs and she sometimes sways when she walks down the backsteps into the yard. Her weight is staying constant, but her visits to the toilet area are becoming more frequent. You often surprise her when you approach, which makes you believe her hearing isn't what it used to be. All those changes support your decision for increasing her visits to her veterinarian.

Note: At 10 or 12 years of age, her health should be professionally reevaluated at least twice a year.

Aging Problems

A geriatric physical will include the usual examination but will concentrate on aging problems. Your veterinarian palpates her joints for arthritic changes and looks into her eyes

Akita's are most comfortable in the house with their family.

with an ophthalmoscope, checking for lens changes. He examines her skin, looking for cysts and tumors that require attention, and checks her mouth for dental disease and tumors. You consult with the clinician about her diet and he or she collects a urine sample to diagnose kidney and bladder health. He or she suggests a blood screen and takes a sample that might reveal liver, kidney, or pancreatic problems.

After the physical is done and the laboratory results are in, the veterinarian announces that Spirit is as healthy as her age allows. At present, she will require no prescription medication, or special diets. The doctor notes that she is developing nuclear sclerosis that appears like cataracts on both eyes. That will mean that

your furniture should remain in its present places to protect Spirit from bumping into it and hurting herself.

The veterinarian suggests an over-the-counter pain reliever for her arthritic joints and advises you to physically help her arise from lying positions.

Callus Care

Spirit spends most of her time on the lawn or carpet but she has nevertheless developed hard dry calluses because she sometimes flops down on the tile. Bruises and calluses form at the points of contact with the hard floor but they generally aren't a serious health problem unless they crack and become infected. You noticed those unsightly formations first on the outside of her elbows. Later they formed on her hocks, sides of her feet, and over her hip bones. You have been rubbing in lanolin and vitamin E ointments every few days to keep them soft and pliable. Your veterinarian notes that if those products don't do the job, a keratolytic cream might work better. He or she tells you that if a callus becomes smelly and infected or swollen, it will require further investigation and treatment.

The best callus therapy is padding. Buy half a dozen bath mats at yard sales or thrift shops and spread a mat in each of Spirit's favorite resting places.

Extra Water Pans

Her kidney function is only slightly compromised, based on the urinalysis and blood screen, but no evidence of bladder infection was found. The clinician suggests that you furnish more water bowls to be sure that she can always get a drink without a long walk. Urinary control problems are common in aged dogs and if urine seeps when she sleeps, those rubber-backed rugs that were bought for her comfort will also absorb any urine leakage that occurs.

Deafness and Lameness

Unfortunately, nothing is to be done for her deafness except to stomp your foot when nearing her napping place to let her know you are in the area. You can lift her posterior to take the strain off her hind legs when she struggles to get up and you might build Spirit a ramp to the back porch so she won't need to negotiate the steps.

When It Is Time to Give Up

Euthanasia is a hard word to say. Your common sense and the advice of your veterinarian will tell you when Spirit is miserable and life holds no further comfort or joy for her. When that time arrives, and it will arrive, you won't be prepared. You won't be ready to give up your devoted and loyal friend but in your heart you will know that it is time. You were always in her corner, helped her up when she fell, and comforted her when she was ill. She depends on you but the decision is yours.

Euthanasia

The intravenous injection causes only a tiny sting when the needle penetrates the skin. The injection is painless and causes Spirit to drift off into a sound sleep from which she will never awaken. Make it as easy for her as you can. Ask your veterinarian to come to your home so that Spirit doesn't have to face a trip

Old Akitas thrive on sound, logical care.

to the hospital. Stay with her while the veterinarian gently holds her foot, raises the vein, and makes the injection.

Saying Good-bye

Ask your veterinarian for the name of a support group to help you deal with your grief. You will never forget Spirit, but you can remember her in her youth by thumbing through the photo album on your coffee table. Donate a tree to a nearby park or plant one in your yard and attach her dog tag to it as a remembrance of the life and years of loyal companionship of a wonderful friend, your Akita.

Books

American Kennel Club. *The Complete Dog Book*, 18th Edition. New York, NY: Simon & Schuster Macmillan Company, 1992.

Coile, Caroline D. *Encyclopedia of Dog Breeds.* Hauppauge, NY: Barron's Educational Series, Inc., 1998.

Beaver, Bonnie V. *Canine Behavior.* Philadelphia, PA: W.B. Saunders Company, 1999.

Bouyet, Barbara. *Akita, Treasure of Japan.* Montecito, CA: M.I.P. Publishing Co., 1992.

Linderman and Funk. *The Complete Akita.* New York: Macmillan Publishing Co., 1983.

Mitchell, Gerald and Kath. *Book of the Breed. The Akita.* Letchworth Herts, England: Ring Press Books, Ltd., 1990.

Rice, Dan. *Big Dog Breeds.* Hauppauge, NY: Barron's Educational Series, Inc., 2001.

Yamazaki, Tetsu and Kojima, Toyoharu. *Legacy of the Dog.* San Francisco, CA: Chronicle Books, 1995.

Web Sites

Akita Club of America
www.akitaclub.org

American Kennel Club
www.akc.org/breeds/akita/index.cfm

Canine Eye Registry Foundation (CERF)
www.cerf.org

Orthopedic Foundation for Animals (OFA)
www.offa.org

University of Pennsylvania Hip Improvement Program (PennHIP)
www.pennhip.org

Exercise behind a secure fence enhances good nutrition.

Akitas can be a great fit for any family.

INDEX

About the Author

Dan Rice is a retired veterinarian from Colorado who continues to pursue his lifelong writing avocation. He revised the *Akita Pet Owner's Manual* because new ideas, techniques, and products have been developed during the 10 years since the first edition was written. He has written more than a dozen Barron's titles presently in print, the last being *Bullmastiffs*.

Acknowledgments

Thanks go out to the exceptional staff at Barron's for allowing me to contribute my efforts to their success, especially to editor Marcy Rosenbaum who guided me through the new format of books in this series and advised me along the way. I am once again, indebted to my lovely wife Marilyn for keeping me focused and for her excellent proofreading.

Important Note

This pet owner's guide tells the reader how to buy and care for an Akita dog. The author and the publisher consider it important to point out that the advice given in this book is meant primarily for normally developed puppies from a good breeder—that is, dogs of excellent physical health and good character.

Anyone who adopts a fully grown dog should be aware that the animal has already formed its basic impressions of human beings. The new owner should watch the animal carefully, including its behavior toward humans, and should meet the previous owner. If the dog comes from a shelter, it may be possible to get some information on the dog's background and peculiarities there. There are dogs that, as a result of bad experiences with humans, behave in an unnatural manner or may even bite. Only people that have experience with dogs should take in such animals.

Caution is further advised in the association of children with dogs, in meeting with other dogs, and in exercising the dog without a leash.

Even well-behaved and carefully supervised dogs sometimes do damage to someone else's property or cause accidents. It is therefore in the owner's interest to be adequately insured against such eventualities, and we strongly urge all dog owners to purchase a liability policy that covers their dog.

Photo Credits

Norvia Behling: page 54; Kent Dannen: pages 2–3, 5, 6, 10, 13, 23, 26, 31, 32, 33, 34, 37, 41, 46, 51, 53, 60TL, 61, 76, 82; Tara Darling: pages 14, 79, 87; Cheryl Ertelt: pages 45, 59, 60TR; Isabelle Francais: pages 4, 8, 9, 15, 17, 18, 19, 20, 25, 28, 35, 36, 38, 40, 42, 43, 44, 48, 49, 50, 55, 56, 57, 58, 64, 66, 67TR, 70, 71, 72, 74, 84, 86, 90, 91, 92, 93; Pets by Paulette: pages 7, 21, 39, 65, 67TL, 83, 88, 89.

Cover Photos

Kent Dannen: inside front cover; Isabelle Francais: front cover, inside back cover; Pets by Paulette: back cover.

All inquiries should be addressed to:
Barron's Educational Series, Inc.
250 Wireless Boulevard
Hauppauge, NY 11788
www.barronseduc.com

ISBN-13: 978-0-7641-3642-9
ISBN-10: 0-7641-3642-9

Library of Congress Catalog Card No. 2006032247

Library of Congress Cataloging-in-Publication Data
Rice, Dan, 1933–
    Akitas : everything about purchase, care, nutrition, behavior, and training / Dan F. Rice.
        p. cm.
    Includes index.
    ISBN-13: 978-0-7641-3642-9
    ISBN-10: 0-7641-3642-9
    1. Akita dog. I. Title.

SF429.A65R53   2007
636.73—dc22   2006032247

Printed in China
9 8 7 6 5 4 3 2 1